Praise for *Tog...*

Struggling with your Bible reading? Little [...] your feet? Carrie brings the prescription for biblical illiteracy to our homes in this fantastic, fun read. Her warm and personal writing style is filled with real life reality, but presses you on to hunger for the Word.

—DANNAH GRESH, bestselling author and founder of
Secret Keeper Girl

For every mom who is drowning in a sea of guilt about your own spiritual walk, this book is your life raft. *Together* presents the radical notion that spending time in the Word is best done as a family activity, instead of in quiet moments of peaceful tranquility. For every mom who can't find a quiet moment to think, much less memorize Scripture, this holistic, manageable, family-friendly approach is exactly what you need to get into the Word and get the Word into you. In a style that is witty, transparent, and engaging, Carrie Ward is just the everyday mama you need to show you that growing in your faith is possible and attainable even amidst the chaos of the little years.

—ERIN DAVIS, author of *Beyond Bath Time: Embracing
Motherhood as a Sacred Role*

I wholeheartedly recommend *Together* on every level—as a friend of Carrie and her family (they're the real deal!), as a story lover (this one will make you laugh and cry), and as a girl who grew up with parents reading the Bible to me daily (the impact has been incalculable). Trust me, you won't be disappointed by this read, and it just might change you and your family forever!

— PAULA HENDRICKS, blogger TrueWoman.com

Together! Growing Appetites for God isn't theoretical, it's practical, born from the real-life experience of Carrie Ward, an ordinary mom with an extraordinary desire to know God's Word and share it with her children. Carrie lets us peek in on both the joys and struggles of pursuing a fresh encounter with Christ and His Word, as she read through the entire Bible aloud to her four children, one chapter and one day at a time. Beleaguered parents (and not just moms, mind you!) who desperately want to "raise their kids right," but sometimes find themselves weary with well-doing and flustered with the plethora of parental advice on the market, will discover in this book a refreshing and liberating simplicity. Many things can distract us, but one thing is necessary: sitting at Jesus' feet to hear His Word. Carrie's story will challenge, encourage, and inspire you—it will even make you laugh out loud! I'm grateful for the unique and valuable contribution this book makes to Christian parents today.

—Brian Hedges, author of *Christ Formed in You*,
Lead Pastor of Fulkerson Park Baptist Church

"MAMA, I'm hungry!!" What mother hasn't heard that from her children? But how much more important is it for us, as mothers, to hear our children say, "Mama, I'm hungry for God." How can we instill in our children a desire to know God and to love His Word? In this book, Carrie teaches us, in very practical and biblical ways, how to stimulate an appetite in our little ones for the things that matter most. I so wish this book had been available when I was raising my four children. But I praise God that a generation of children today will be blessed because of Carrie's tender and insightful instruction on how to grow our children closer to Him.

—Janet Parshall, nationally syndicated talk show host
Janet Parshall *In the Market with Janet Parshall*
Host/Executive Producer

I am so inspired and challenged by Carrie's book. I hope you have an appetite for spiritual growth and authentic intimacy with God. Be ready to "digest" this wonderful, practical book.

—Karen Loritts, speaker. teacher, and author

Like all Christian parents we long to raise our children "in the fear and discipline of the Lord." Carrie's wonderful little book models one simple but profoundly important way we can do that—reading God's Word together. *Together* has strengthened our resolve to maintain this important discipline and it has encouraged us to see that it is not only possible, but that it bears fruit.

—Tim and Aileen Challies

Together

Growing Appetites for God

Carrie Ward

MOODY PUBLISHERS

CHICAGO

Edited by Annette LaPlaca
Interior design: Ragont Design
Cover design: Maralynn Rochat
Cover image: Birds & Texture–iStock
Author photo: Katie Bollinger

Library of Congress Cataloging-in-Publication Data

Ward, Carrie.
    Together : growing appetites for God / Carrie Ward.
        p. cm.
    ISBN 978-0-8024-0448-0
    1. Bible—Reading. I. Title.
    BS617.W26 2012
    220.071—dc23

                        2011050076

We hope you enjoy this book from Moody Publishers. Our goal is to provide high-quality, thought-provoking books and products that connect truth to your real needs and challenges. For more information on other books and products written and produced from a biblical perspective, go to www.moodypublishers. com or write to:

Moody Publishers
820 N. LaSalle Boulevard
Chicago, IL 60610

3 5 7 9 10 8 6 4 2

Printed in the United States of America

To my best friend, Wes,
Thank you for being a godly, loving, fun,
exceptional husband and father.
I love you.

To my other favorite people,
Graham, Maggie, Benjamin and Emma,
You are gifts from God. You bring
immeasurable love and joy to my life.
I'm so happy to be on this journey with you.
I love you.

The law of the Lord is perfect,
restoring the soul;
The testimony of the Lord is sure,
making wise the simple.
The precepts of the Lord are right,
rejoicing the heart;
The commandment of the Lord is pure,
enlightening the eyes.
The fear of the Lord is clean, enduring forever;
The judgments of the Lord are true;
they are righteous altogether.
They are more desirable than gold,
yes, than much fine gold;
Sweeter also than honey and the
drippings of the honeycomb.

Psalm 19:7–10

Contents

Foreword

*I*n a recent interview for a magazine article, I was asked: "What impact did the Bible have on your coming to faith in Christ, and what impact has it had on your growth as a disciple?" To which I quickly responded: "Everything!"

I can't thank the Lord enough for the blessing of having grown up in a Word-saturated environment. My parents loved the Lord and it showed. They modeled a high view of Scripture; they were consistently in the Word themselves and sought to make it a part of the fabric of our home life. Plus, they gave us plenty of positive exposure to others who loved Christ and honored His Word.

Those early experiences of learning God's Word and (so important!) seeing it lived out, gave me a priceless gift that has been with me all of my life: *an appetite for God.*

The fact is, we all have appetites. I am deeply grateful for the ways my parents helped to foster in us an appetite for what really satisfies . . . Him! More than anything else, they wanted each of their seven children to know and love God; so they made sure our lives were planted in His Word. It's not that we talked about the Bible all the time or that our family perfectly lived up to its ideals—we didn't. Yet they were intentional in their efforts to make our home revolve around the Lord and His Word. I am still reaping the benefits every day of my life—still hungry for God, and eager to cultivate that appetite in others.

Regardless of your spiritual upbringing, if your hunger for God isn't what you wish it was, if you desire for your children to have a life-long passion for God and His Word . . . read on.

For sure, spiritual appetites can't be forced. Parents can't make their children want to walk with God; God has to turn on the light in their hearts and draw them to Himself. But there is much that parents (and caring friends) can do to create an atmosphere conducive to spiritual growth, and to nurture in their children a desire to know and prize Christ.

Carrie Ward was a young mom with two "little ones" when our lives first intersected. A dozen years later, there are four school age children, the oldest of whom stands a head taller than his mom. In that span of time, it has been a joy to watch Carrie develop an insatiable appetite for God, and then to see the journey God has taken this family on, as she has been the impetus, together with her husband Wes, to "salt the oats" to help make their children thirsty for God.

The last chapter has not been written in the lives of the Ward children—or in any of our lives for that matter. This is a journey, the final destination of which will not be reached in this life. But I know that a foundation is being laid in the hearts of Graham, Maggie, Benjamin, and Emma, that is going to stand them in good stead for the rest of their lives. I do not believe they will easily be able to forsake the God they have been growing to know and love while sitting around the kitchen table day after day with their mom and an open Bible.

What God has done and is doing in Wes and Carrie's family is unusual—but that's not because they are some special breed of Christian, or have some secret ingredient available to them that is inaccessible to others. I believe God wants to bless your family with a fresh measure of His presence and grace. The book you hold in your hand will inspire and encourage you to be more intentional in seeking Him—as a parent and together as a family.

NANCY LEIGH DEMOSS

Introduction: Not-so-Quiet Times

[Jesus] said, "It is written:
'Man shall not live on bread alone,
but on every word that proceeds from
the mouth of God.'" Matthew 4:4

*O*n a wintery Monday morning, my kids and I were reading in 2 Kings 3 the account of the king of Israel, the king of Judah, and the king of Edom joining forces to battle against the Moabites. There's a great story here of how God provided water for these armies, but here's the verse that stopped our reading:

> Now all the Moabites had heard that the kings had come to fight against them; so every man, young and old, who could bear arms was called up and stationed on the border. (2 Kings 3:21 NIV)

My youngest daughter, Emma, asked, "What does it mean, all 'who could bear arms'?"

I replied, "It means anyone who could handle a gun."

Not realizing what I had just said, I went on with the reading. All my children were looking at me with puzzled expressions when my youngest son, Benjamin, articulated the question on everyone's mind: "They had *guns* in the Bible?"

My head hit the table. My kids burst into laughter. I mumbled from my hunched-over position, "No, they did not have guns in the Bible." They laughed even louder, and I joined in.

When I gained my composure, I started again with verse 22.

When they got up early in the morning, the sun was shining on the water. To the Moabites across the way, the water looked red—like blood. "That's blood!" they said. "Those kings must have fought and slaughtered each other. Now to the plunder, Moab!"

But when the Moabites came to the camp of Israel, the Israelites . . ."

"Saw their guns!" my oldest son yelled. This sent us into another round of laughter. Benjamin said, "We laugh a lot when we read the Bible."

It's true. We do spend a lot of time laughing—sometimes over the surprising situations of Scripture, sometimes over the funny remark of one of my children, and sometimes just over

Together

Mom's attempts to read and explain.

There are also moments of tension, excitement, disappointment, and openly displayed awe as we read God's Word. That's one thing I've learned about reading the Bible to children: they don't hold back their emotions. When we read, they react!

Little did I know when I began reading the Bible with my children ten years ago, that all of that energy and display of emotion would breathe new life into my study of God's Word.

NOT TOO LATE . . . AND NOT TOO EARLY

I put my faith in Christ as a child. At a young age, I had a simple understanding of these basic facts: I was born a sinner; my nature is inclined toward sin. God, the Creator of all, establishes that there is punishment for sin. He will judge my sin, and I *should* receive His wrath.

But I have been rescued. God, the judge, extended mercy to me. Even before I was born, even before I had committed the sins God knew I would commit, He provided deliverance. He sent Jesus to earth, and Jesus took my punishment.

Jesus took on human flesh, walked on the earth as I do, and was tempted as I am, yet He did not sin. Jesus lived a perfect life. He did not deserve any punishment. But Jesus performed the ultimate act of love. He stepped into my place and took the penalty I deserved. God, who decreed the punishment for my sin, also took the punishment for my sin.

As a result, I can put my faith and trust and hope in Jesus. I can believe what He did, and the righteous life that He lived can be counted as mine.

With the faith that God gave me, as a child, I believed, and I continue to believe.

Over the years, however, I faced a recurring struggle when it came to reading God's Word. I was taught how important it is to read Scripture on my own, and I knew this was true. I was shown numerous techniques and methods for studying the Word. But when it came time to sit down and read my Bible, I tried and failed.

My acceptance by God was (and is) by grace alone through faith alone. My acceptance is not based on whether or not I have read the entire Bible. However, as the years went by, I became increasingly aware that my maturity as a follower of Christ was being affected by my lack of knowledge of God's Word.

I tended to repeat the same cycle. First, there would come a challenge of some sort to read my Bible daily, and I would think, *This time I'm going to do it.*

I'd start off strong and optimistic, reading every day for a week (maybe two). Then the Bible reading was choked out by other things, until

YOU'RE NEVER too old and never too young to hear God speak.

the attempt eventually fizzled all together.

The Bible seemed so big and difficult to understand, at times even boring. My self-discipline wasn't strong enough. My attention span wasn't long enough. My sense of Christian duty was not robust enough to maintain the reading long-term. Each attempt to read the Bible was clouded by guilt, frustration, and the seemingly inevitable failure.

All around me, Christians seemed to have mastered this discipline. Why couldn't I? I was beginning to think it was too late for me.

Before you start to get caught up in what sounds like despair, let me assure you, this is a story of hope—marvelous hope! When I was thirty-six years old, God gave me a new, fresh, strong desire to read His Word.

And God didn't just give me a desire, He gave me a plan.

The plan was clear. I was to read the entire Bible *with* my preschool children.

You might be thinking that trying to read the whole Bible to preschoolers would hold me back in my study of God and His Word. Or you may be thinking that my Bible reading would be, at best, chaotic.

Well, I won't tell you my Bible study time has been quiet! But God used these fun, energetic, spontaneous, and insightful little people to make His Word come alive to me. I have learned more about God with this small community than I would ever have learned on my own. And, not only that, this discipline that once was a struggle for me has become the joy of getting to know God.

Do you want to have consistent time in God's Word? It's not too late. Do you want to get the Word of God into the hearts and minds of your children? It's not too early for them to hear God speak. My prayer is that God will use our testimony to awaken in you the belief that it is possible to consistently read and study the Bible. I am confident God can grow in you and your children a hunger for—and a great delight in—His Word.

Augustine said, "When we read Scripture, God speaks to us." I can say with confidence that you're never too old and, as our story will tell, never too young to hear God speak.

We're reading God's Word, and He is speaking to us.

We Read the Bible:
And It Comes to Life

If anyone has ears to hear,
let him hear. Mark 4:23

*O*n the day I started out to read the entire Bible with my three children, I was euphoric. This was going to be great. I sat down at breakfast and read, "In the beginning God created . . ." Somehow, naively, I expected my children, the oldest of them only four years old, to share my enthusiasm. I expected them to be filled with wonder. I expected them to be wowed by the reading of God's Word. I expected them . . . to listen. What was I thinking?

My first three mornings went something like this.

"*'Thus the heavens and the earth were completed, and all their hosts.'*"

"Can I have some more toast?"

"Uh sure, just a second. *'By the seventh day God completed His work which He had done, and He rested on the seventh day from all His work which He had done.'*"

"Are we gonna have to take a nap today?"

"Yes! God rested, and so should you. Where was I? *'Then God blessed the seventh day and sanctified it, because in it—'* Where are you going?"

"I need to wash my hands."

"Can you wait just a minute?"

"Sticky! I'm sticky!"

It was a scene made for YouTube. While I was reading about the fall of man, my little ones were spinning in their chairs, standing in their chairs, and asking questions not at all related to Adam and Eve. I thought, *I am reading out loud to myself.* This might not have been a bad thing, but it was not exactly what I had in mind.

Our trip through the Bible began with me wondering what in the world I had undertaken. Could I do this without lots of pictures? Would they ever be able to listen, or at least be still—or even just be quiet? God was merciful, and He did not leave me in this predicament for long.

On day four I reached the story of Cain and Abel. Mind you, while I read, the children were as wiggly and talkative as ever. The story was chopped in pieces as I stopped to answer unrelated questions or jumped up to get more food.

Once the reading and waffles were behind us, I sent Graham and Maggie off to play in the living room while I began cleaning up. But before I finished clearing the dishes from the table, I realized what it was they were playing. They were "playing" Cain and Abel.

I watched them take turns playing the part of Cain. They would walk off in the "field" together, and Cain would whack Abel over the head with some sort of invisible farm implement. This may not sound like the sort of interaction a mom should be excited to see between her children, but I was thrilled. They were listening! Whether or not they intended to listen, they had definitely *heard* the story in great detail.

From that point on, I didn't obsess over trying to get them to hang on every word. I did try to teach them to sit still, be quiet, and pay attention, but each morning as they were smacking, squirming, and blurting, I knew they were also hearing. They were hearing the Word of God. This was what I wanted, because if I could read God's Word and they would hear it, God could use it to change their hearts. This was the encouragement I needed to keep going. And keep going we did.

Reenactments of the Cain and Abel variety became

an almost daily occurrence. Biblical epics became commonplace in the Ward living room, our standard After-Breakfast Theater. Stuffed animals were gathered by twos and led into the ark (a blanket draped over the dining room chairs). Abraham and Isaac climbed the mountain, and Isaac was incredibly thankful for the ram. Joseph was sold into slavery. Moses threw off his sandals in front of the burning bush. Joshua marched around Jericho. I waited with much anticipation to see how my children would interpret each day's Bible reading.

One day a man of God came to Jeroboam to speak a word against the altars and idols that Jeroboam had built.

> Now when the king heard the saying of the man of God, which he cried against the altar in Bethel, Jeroboam stretched out his hand from the altar, saying, "Seize him." But his hand which he stretched out against him dried up, so that he could not draw it back to himself. The altar also was split apart and the ashes were poured out from the altar, according to the sign which the man of God had given by the word of the Lord. The king said to the man of God, "Please entreat the Lord your God, and pray for me, that my hand may be restored to me." So the man of God entreated the Lord, and the king's hand was restored to him, and it became as it was before. (1 Kings 13:4–6)

This story captivated my children. All day, and into the next, my little people ran around the house yelling, "Seize him!" Then one itty-bitty hand would wither. (It was interesting to watch a preschool interpretation of one's hand drying up. It reminded me of the shrinking of the Wicked Witch in *The Wizard of Oz*. They would pull their hands to their chest and then sort of scrunch up in a ball on the floor. It was more like their whole bodies had withered.) After that, a three-foot-tall "man" of God would pray, and the little hand would be restored. It was great. Even my hand withered (and was promptly healed) a few times.

By the time we got to stories of David, the acting had become quite skillful. Goliath stood on a chair to be more "Goliathy" and yelled, "Am I a dog?" I fed David a line, "I come to you in the name of the Lord." Then David made one adept swing of his slingshot. Goliath died several times that day, always dramatically.

Another day David was playing his harp when Saul threw a spear at him (or was it her?).

David hid by the stone (a basket) wait-

 **MY SON** the pharaoh jumped to his feet and shouted a command to his servant: "After them!"

ing for Jonathan to shoot his arrows.

In the cavelike closet, David crept up behind Saul to cut a piece from his robe (bathrobe).

The acting was larger than life—and hilarious. I loved it! God created children with a wonderful imagination and a great capacity for playing pretend. My children didn't just hear the account given in the Bible; they put themselves in the story. Along with the fun, something significant was happening. The Lord was reinforcing what we had read. Their play not only reinforced God's Word in their minds, but in my mind as well.

From the beginning I had been praying that God would help them remember and understand more than I thought they were capable of. And as we moved through the Old Testament, God continued to reinforce His Word to our children. I saw this at work on a grand scale the day we read Psalm 105.

A portion of this psalm recounts the story of the children of Israel being brought out of Egypt with wondrous signs. This triggered their memory of Moses confronting the pharaoh. When the eating and reading were over, the acting began.

My older son, Graham, seized the role of Pharaoh sitting in his thronelike leather chair. Benjamin was now old enough to participate, but on this particular morning he was more like a guard in the pharaoh's palace, watching the story unfold. Emma, our newest arrival, must have been playing the part of an Egyptian baby—too young to appreciate the drama. Maggie, three, was Pharaoh's trusted servant.

I leaned over the kitchen counter, completely captivated but trying not to be spotted for fear they might stop the performance.

"Bring him in," declared Pharaoh in a demanding tone.

Maggie, the servant, quickly ushered in an *invisible* Moses. (The invisible Moses was an interesting twist.)

There was a muffled conversation between the pharaoh and the invisible Moses. Pharaoh suddenly became quite agitated and yelled, "No! Send him away." At this, the servant hastily escorted invisible Moses out of the presence of Pharaoh.

After a quiet moment Pharaoh began to shout in alarm, "Oh, oh, blood, blood!" and then an urgent "Go get him." The servant wasted no time in retrieving Moses.

Hushed whispers were exchanged, and again, Pharaoh grew agitated. "No!" he exclaimed, and Moses was again sent out of the palace.

There was a brief silence before Pharaoh howled, "Oh, oh, frogs, frogs! Bring me Moses!" Moses reappeared (tricky for an invisible Bible character, mind you!), accompanied by Pharaoh's faithful servant, of course.

I wondered if the children were actually going to remember all ten plagues. However, without any planning on their part, they condensed the story and skipped right to the end.

Once again there was a conversation between Pharaoh and "Moses," but in the end the pharaoh yelled the inevitable "No!" and out went Moses. At this point Pharaoh, with a surprising amount of sincerity, cried out, "My son, my son!" as he (apparently) saw his lifeless first-born. This time the pharaoh told his servant to go and inform Moses that he and his people could leave Egypt. So Maggie went to one side of the room, made a grand sweeping motion with her arms, and yelled, "You can go."

Oh, but the story didn't end there! A moment later, my son the pharaoh jumped to his feet and shouted a command to his servant: "After them!" The pharaoh and his servant began the chase, through the living room and the kitchen, around the corner to the dining room, and back to the living room. By the time they reached the living room the second time, Pharaoh was yelling, "They're crossing the Red Sea. Let's go after them!" Then, at one end of the living room, he collapsed, giving a great performance of a drowning man.

However, his servant did not remember accurately all the details of the story, and she kept running. My son popped his head up and yelled, "No, Maggie, you have to stop. You drown in the water."

My daughter didn't really like this idea. With a confused expression, she looked to me for the answer. I said, "Yes, Maggie, if you're with the pharaoh, you drown in the sea."

With an awfully serious look on her face, she said, "Can we play this again? Next time I'll be Moses."

As my children have grown, the performances of Living Room Bible Theater have become less frequent, although it occasionally recurs spontaneously. But how thankful I am for those rich Old Testament accounts! I'm so thankful for little children and the sense of wonder they express. I am thankful for the way God made their minds like little sponges, soaking up details that I sometimes overlook. I'm thankful for those days of rehearsing Bible stories in our living room. I have watched my children remember, and help each other remember, passages in remarkable detail. As our reading continued, God also answered my prayer that they would understand.

I praise God for the way I have witnessed His Word being implanted in the minds of my children. But before we ever started this Bible reading adventure, God got my attention and did a work in my own heart.

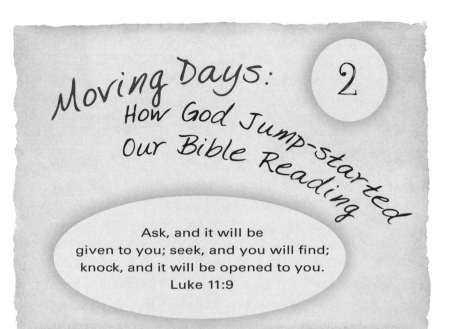

Moving Days:
How God Jump-started
Our Bible Reading

2

Ask, and it will be
given to you; seek, and you will find;
knock, and it will be opened to you.
Luke 11:9

*M*oving day! You watch total strangers load your worldly possessions into a large truck. You may feel uneasy as they drive away with your stuff, but you have no time to linger, worrying if your wedding dishes will make it or not. After you wave good-bye to those guys with your belongings, you spend the next few hours trying to force fit into your car all those "keepsakes" you wouldn't entrust to the movers—along with the broom and dustpan. Thankfully, we had two cars!

Our big day had come. Once all the surplus items had been squeezed in, we situated our most precious cargo, our two children, and said "good-bye" to Chicago on our way to Little Rock. In some ways this was a big move for us, but it was actually a pretty easy one. We were excited to be buying our first house. My husband, Wes, was energized about his new job on the broadcast team at FamilyLife Today. And, having grown up in Texas and Oklahoma, we were both eager to be moving back closer to family and friends.

We drove all night and arrived at our new home the next morning, just in time to watch those same strangers, now most trustworthy men, unload all our stuff. Our well-rested children ran from room to room while we tried to stay awake to oversee the work and do some cleaning. You can imagine the scene—boxes piled high, the faint smell of Comet and fresh paint in the air.

Those first few weeks in Little Rock were spent doing the normal stuff, surveying what had gotten mangled in the move and what hadn't, reconnecting with friends nearby, and eating out way too often. Right in the middle of getting our new nest in order, I received some troubling news from dear friends of ours. I was floored. It was the kind of news that makes you weak in the knees and leaves you with a persistent anxious feeling. The chaos I had been facing on the outside, I was now experiencing inside.

That first night I cried and prayed. In the days that followed I tried to learn every possible solution to this problem. I thought there must be something I could do or say that would mend the situation.

But at the end of each day, I did the only thing I knew I could do: I prayed. I sought God more intently than I had in a long time, perhaps ever.

This news drove me to a desperate kind of prayer that lasted several months, and in the process God began to reveal Himself in ways I had not experienced before.

Around this same time, I was "very pregnant" with our third child and felt a bit self-conscious when Wes and I went to dinner with a group from his work. FamilyLife Today and Back to the Bible were talking with Nancy Leigh DeMoss about helping her start a radio program. After a day of meetings, the group and spouses were going out to dinner. As it turned out, Wes and I sat directly across from Nancy. She and I had the opportunity to chat throughout the evening, and this conversation launched a friendship that God immediately began to use in our lives.

When Wes came home from work the next day, he had a gift for me. Nancy had sent me a copy of *A Place of Quiet Rest*, her book about growing close to God through a devotional life. It wasn't too many days later that our son was born. While feeding and holding little Benjamin, I began to read Nancy's book. Wes said I read it like I had a book report due. I couldn't put it down. It was as though Nancy were speaking directly to me, saying just what

 **AS I READ** this book about a devotional life, I became aware of my lack of devotion.

I needed to hear, in just the right words and at just the right time. She had no idea, but God did.

Amazingly, the words Nancy had written were an answer to my prayers. For months I had been crying out to God for help. Now He was answering my cry. Not the way I expected—or even the way I wanted. God lovingly began to show me more about Him and—gulp!—more about me.

As I read this book about a devotional life, I became aware of my lack of devotion. I began to realize that my sin was hideous and grievous to a holy and good God. However, to my shame, I was not up nights crying and praying about *my* condition.

In God's providence, just after my encounter with Nancy and *A Place of Quiet Rest*, we joined a church where the pastor was beginning a series on the fear of God. His main text was Proverbs 1:7, but for several weeks he swept through the whole of Scripture pointing out what the Bible has to say about fearing God. He emphasized that we should all have a holy fear and a healthy dread of the living God.

After weeks of hearing what the Bible had to say about the fear of God, I was given a renewed sense of awe. I can remember standing in church holding back tears as we sang songs about the glory of God. I was flooded with the reality that this great God deserves reverence and worship. Jesus, my Savior, deserves my devotion.

AHA!

Break up your fallow ground, for it is time to seek the Lord until He comes to rain righteousness on you. Hosea 10:12

God was working in my life, and in the life of my friends. He was using this difficult time to jackhammer my heart, making me more open and receptive to Him. He had driven me to seek Him deeply in prayer. In His great timing, He worked through Nancy's book to remind me of my sinful nature and my need to be devoted to Christ. Then through that same book and the faithful preaching of the Word, I was given a fresh perspective on my relationship with this holy God. I am thankful that God also gave me my husband, Wes, to walk me through this time and be my living example. He cried with me, prayed with me, answered a lot of questions, and made me laugh. (I needed that.)

We sometimes refer to those times in life when we finally understand a concept as "aha" moments. Frankly, at this point, I was having so many aha moments that I wanted to throw up my hands and say, "Stop! I can't take any more."

But God didn't stop. Little did I know, this was just the beginning. God had much more in store.

THE DISTRACTION FAST

Let us also lay aside every encumbrance . . .
and run with with endurance the race that is
set before us. Hebrews 12:1

Do you ever get distracted? I do. (You may think I'm distracted right now, but I am heading somewhere with this.) Sometimes, try as I might to focus on one thing, I am easily swept away by something unrelated. In a heartbeat I'm off making a mental to-do list, thinking about the next activity, or, even worse, having an argument in my mind with a person who upset me the day before. I'm embarrassed to admit how often my mind wanders from the subject at hand.

If my own thoughts are not enough to distract me,

SOMETIMES we are so busy with what's urgent that we don't accomplish what's important.

plenty of external things can capture my attention. In college I heard a lecture on "the tyranny of the urgent." Sometimes we are so busy with what's urgent that we don't accomplish what's important. I am often reminded of this when I check email. I think that my email is urgent: "I need to know if so and so responded to my message." However, I sometimes neglect the important (interacting with my children, for example) for the urgent (checking my email). Frequently that bit of correspondence is not even close to being "urgent"; it's just my curiosity leading me to believe it can't wait. When I give in to curiosity, email is a distraction from the important things I know I should be doing.

Facebook is another tempting distraction. I have a Facebook account, and I appreciate the *idea* of immediately connecting with "friends." But I don't get on Facebook too often because I learned early on what can happen. You think to yourself, *I'll check in and see what my friends are saying. I'll quickly come up with some clever status. Oh, and I want to look at those pictures that were just posted.* The problem is you don't actually think; you just do it. All of a sudden—zap!—an hour has passed, and your kids are sort of wandering aimlessly waiting for you to surface.

One thing is certain in life: distractions abound.

Several years ago, Wes and I were on a flight to California, seated in the front row of the coach section. During takeoff a flight attendant took her spot in the jump seat facing us. Wes loves to ask questions of strangers—a *gazillion* questions. So as we all got buckled in and ready for the plane to take off, Wes began: "How many flights have you been on this week?" "Where have you traveled today?" "Where do you live?" "How often do you get to be at home?" "Do you like your job?" "What is life like for you?" As she began to open up, this young woman revealed to us that she kept her TV on all day, every day, *even when she wasn't at home.* She explained that, being a single woman, the noise of the TV was a welcome "distraction" from the quiet of living alone.

I had not really thought of television as a distraction. It was just a customary part of life. We all watch plenty of TV, don't we?

I once worked with a young woman from Germany who was in the United States studying for her master's degree. During one lecture, the professor made a reference to the Beverly Hillbillies. Everyone seemed to understand his illustration except my German friend, so she raised her hand and asked, "Who are the Beverly Hillbillies?" Immediately, and in remarkable unison, the entire class began to sing the theme song from the TV show *The Beverly Hillbillies*. Jed's ballad never sounded finer. She was amazed! Not only did the entire class know *about* the Beverly Hillbillies, the entire class had the theme song memorized.

As she relayed the story to me, I broke into my own solo rendition of the song. Impressive, isn't it? We *all* grew up with the TV on a lot, right? It's just the norm, isn't it?

The families Wes and I spent time with all logged in their weekly hours of TV, and we were content to follow that model. We tried to avoid programs that would cause temptation or lead us in an unbiblical worldview, but we were definitely a TV-watching family. I had developed the habit of clicking on the television for the kids in the morning, and we watched as a family at night. It was an easy and fun habit. However, we were on the verge of an epiphany.

FamilyLife Today was preparing to air an interview with Bob DeMoss regarding his book *T.V.: The Great Escape!* (Crossway). Dennis

 **I FIGURED I HAD** probably already frittered away three years of my life.

Rainey led his staff by challenging them to take a thirty-one-day media fast to coincide with the release of these programs. Wes and I talked about this challenge and knew it was the right thing to do. We were strong enough to go a month without CNN and Big Bird, right? The truth was, we knew that this box in the living room was a focal point in our home and it would be good for us to look away for a while. So we said yes to the challenge.

When the time drew near, we did wonder if we could make it through the thirty-one days. We didn't *need* TV, but it's safe to say we liked it, and it seemed to be helpful with three small children. At that time our older son was three. Graham was born with the ability to zone out in front of any program and forget he had a family in the room. Maggie was two and more of a come-and-go watcher. Benjamin was a mere four months old. While the older two were watching TV in the morning, I could give Benjamin some attention and get a few things done around the house. The idea of a TV fast made me wonder how I would get everything done *and* keep all my children "entertained." Not to mention that Wes and I were going to miss tracking with our favorite shows in the evening.

I decided it would be a good idea for me to prepare for this fast by reading *T.V.: The Great Escape!* It was quite an eye-opener. Bob DeMoss wrote about the crazy amount of time that average Americans spend watching television. (When he wrote the book, Americans watched about three hours a day. New stats indicate that viewing hours are now up to four hours each day—and that doesn't even take into account recreational screen time in front of computers, tablets, and smartphones.) But let's say you watched just the three hours a day. If you start this habit when you are five years old and continue until you're sixty-five, and you watch fifty weeks out of the year (assuming you take an occasional TV vacation), you will end up watching TV for more than seven years of your life! Imagine giving *seven years* of your life to news, talent shows, and sitcoms (or worse—"reality" TV). DeMoss points out that, among other things, you could earn a master's degree in seven years. By this time, I figured I had probably already frittered away three years of my life.

So when August rolled around, we un-plugged our TV. I must admit, even with the sound of my children, there was an awk-ward quietness for the first several days. It was tempting to turn the TV back on for noise, if nothing else. But we kept the television off, and the benefits soon came forth in living color.

The first week I realized that my logic about television entertaining my children had been completely wrong. For the first time, I saw what was really happening in our family as a result of TV. We were actually nurturing Graham's bent to zone out. He would get totally engrossed in whatever was on and completely ignore his family. When the TV was turned off, he discovered he had a sister and she was fun to play with! Meanwhile, I discovered it was a whole lot more satisfying to watch Graham and Maggie play than to watch them watch television.

When Wes came home from work, we ate supper— without the TV—and then we set out for a walk or read a good book or played a game or geared up for the next day. We turned our attention away from the television and toward each other.

We had done so well on this fast that Wes and I decided we'd give the family a reward for good behavior. We still had a bit of an urge to watch something, so during week three we planned a family night of watching home movies. We hadn't even made it through the first recording before Wes and I looked at each other in disbelief. We saw it at the same time: in our home movies *we were watching TV!* If we weren't watching it, it was always on. We laughed, but we were actually stunned to realize just how prominent television had been in our house.

When the fast officially came to an end, we did not run back to our old habit. Wes and I had changed. Before the TV fast, our senses had become dull to the way people talk, the images displayed, and the attitudes revealed on this screen in our living room. By getting away from it for thirty-one days, we suddenly gained a clear view of what we and our children were being exposed to. We would never have condoned those attitudes, behaviors, and speech in ourselves. Why were we allowing them to permeate our home through television?

This fast had another unexpected benefit for me. I tend to be a fearful person, mentally conjuring up all sorts of calamities that might happen. I know other women who face this same struggle. Remember the flight attendant who kept her TV on twenty-four hours a day? She told us that the noise of the television made her feel more secure. I discovered the opposite to be true. The television was actually fueling my fears. News and seemingly harmless dramas were leading my mind to places I should not go. Fear is a real battle and it is not easily eliminated, but when I stopped feeding my mind with TV, my fears decreased as well.

We no longer have a constant hum of the television in our home. We do watch TV, but we choose to watch a specific program or video and then we turn it off. And since there is a strong temptation for us to be distracted by television, we've made it a frequent habit to repeat the media fast—and that includes occasionally breaking away from TV, Internet, video games, and even iPhones.

Being free from the grip of television is important, but the media fast was not just about Wes and me developing willpower. God was at work! Television was a huge distraction. It ate up our time, influenced our minds, and even affected our behavior. It distracted us from God. Wes and I agree that this first fast from media was a pivotal point in our lives. God used this fast to free us from one of the most consuming distractions in our home. He was about to fill us with something much more satisfying.

A NEW HUNGER

Behold, I long for Your precepts; revive me
through Your righteousness. Psalm 119:40

God had shaken up my world a bit. This was good and tiring and humbling. I was gaining a bigger view of God and, along with that, a heightened awareness of my own sin. I was reminded that Jesus bridged a huge gap between God and me.

After the distraction of TV was removed, I would have been happy to take a breather from all this life-changing, habit-altering activity, except for one thing. During these months God was graciously growing in me a hunger for His Word.

I've shared with you my struggle to discipline myself

to study the Bible. The mention of those phrases we use for Bible study and prayer, such as *quiet time* or *devotional life*, left me feeling frustrated, discouraged, and guilty. These old feelings were still present within me, but now the desire to read the Bible was less a sense of Christian duty and more an inner craving. I wanted to get closer to God. And I couldn't wait for the opportunity to sit still and study His Word.

If you're not laughing now, you should be. In case you have forgotten, at that point I had three children, approximately three-and-a-half, two, and five months. How ironic that God was giving me this great yearning to know Him through His Word at the busiest time of my life. I wasn't sure I could have the energy to care for my little people and the attentiveness to truly study the Bible. Nevertheless, I was hungry to hear from God.

I've always heard that it's ideal to start your day with a time of prayer and Bible study. So I—not being a morning person at all—began to work hard (again) at getting up early. However, no matter how early I began, inevitably there came an opportunity for me to be a mom. Right in the middle of my "quiet time" came one, two, or even three little, but loud, voices. They needed me. I encountered a real tension between my desire to study God's Word and my home filled with children with ever-present, legitimate needs. Full days and late nights made early mornings even more difficult, but my desire to get to know God through His Word provided the motivation to keep trying.

Simultaneously, I wanted to get a greater knowledge of the Bible into my children. I had come to the realization that I spent most of my days *reacting* to my children instead of *leading* them. I noticed moms who deliberately guided their children's thinking and actions. I didn't necessarily want to follow their exact methods, but I did admire the fact that they were intentional. I wanted these days with my children to be purposeful, and what I most wanted to teach them was about God and His Word.

As always, God was way ahead of me. Several months before, a friend had given us a book by Marian Schoolland called *Leading Little Ones to God* (Eerdmans). My friend told me, "My father and mother led me through this book when I was a little girl. I *love* giving it to parents of young children." At the time, life just seemed too busy, so I set it on a shelf thinking I would get to it eventually. But in this season of life,

Leading Little Ones to God was exactly what I wanted to do, and the book came down from the shelf.

Wes and I agreed that this would be a great time for me to go through some basics with the kids, and the book would give us a structured activity during the day. So that fall we spent about three months working our way through the lessons in this book. Though it is simple and basic—perhaps *because* it is simple and basic—I found this book to be as good for me as it was for the kids, reminding me of foundational truths about God our Father, Jesus our Savior, and the work of the Holy Spirit. When we finished *Leading Little Ones to God*, I wondered what we would do next. So I began the search for something else to help get God's Word into my children.

All this time, I continued to struggle with my own time of Bible study. Consistency was as difficult as I had always found it to be. I was having trouble getting up in the morning, and when I did get up, it was difficult to patiently work through the interruptions. (Oddly enough, though I'm not a morning person, I have some children who are.) Occasionally I attempted to read the Bible at night in bed, but this never seemed to work. When I woke up with the Bible on my chest, I could barely remember that I had been reading, let alone *what* I had been reading. Before long, I was battling the same old discouragement that had plagued me for years.

I want to be clear that I love being a wife and mom. I consider it a privilege. I love the crazy hum of our home. I have a wonderful husband, and my children are a reward from God. But how could I meet the demands of being a wife and mom and also have time to give real focus to knowing God through His Word? That was my dilemma.

Then one day an idea came to me. I really wanted to succeed in reading the Bible—the *entire* Bible. This was something I had never done. *And* I wanted to get God's Word into the minds and hearts of my children. I thought, *Why not do both at the same time?* There I was searching bookstores for a children's story Bible that had more stories and more text taken directly from Scripture when—*Eureka*! Why not just read them the Bible? Why not read it together?

When the idea had been brewing in my head for a few days, I needed some affirmation. So as Wes and I were getting ready for bed, I said, "I have this idea. I've been thinking about starting something with the kids, and I want to get your opinion.

"You know I want to read the Bible, and we want to teach the kids more about the Bible. So what would you think if I read through the *entire* Bible *with* the kids?"

Without hesitation, Wes immediately said, "Go for it!" His reaction was genuine enthusiasm. Somehow I think he knew that this would be as good for me as it would be for our kids. Yet he couldn't resist asking, "Exactly how are you going to do this?"

I had a plan all worked out. The kids and I could read through the entire Bible together, by reading one chapter of the Bible each morning at breakfast. We could read five days a week, leaving more flexibility on the weekend when Wes was home.

Again his response was total encouragement. However, as I listened to myself explain my idea out loud, I suddenly became curious to know exactly how long it would take us to read through the *entire* Bible. I got out a pencil and piece of paper and began to do the math. I counted the chapters in the Bible and how many days a year we would read. I factored in "sick days," times when we might be sick or out of town and not able to read. I sat in bed doing my math exercise, and when I was finished I started laughing.

I looked at Wes and said, "At one chapter a day, it's going to take us eight years to read through the Bible. Eight years. Yikes!"

To me, not being a terribly disciplined person, this long-term commitment was almost more than my mind could comprehend. I sat quietly for a minute letting the mind-boggling number soak in. Surprisingly, the desire did not go away. I crumpled up that piece of paper, clicked off the light, and said to Wes, "I want to do this anyway."

And so we began.

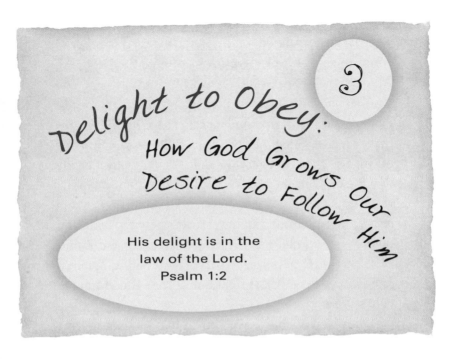

3

Delight to Obey: How God Grows Our Desire to Follow Him

His delight is in the
law of the Lord.
Psalm 1:2

I've heard that it takes twenty-one days to form a habit. Reading the Bible at breakfast quickly became a habit for us. Now, if for some reason I sit down at breakfast without first getting my Bible, one of the kids will jump up to get it and set it on the table by my spot. They know we are going to read.

At some point along the way, I developed another habit. I give a little teaser regarding what we are going to read the next day. The day we finished Joel, I said, "Tomorrow we start the book of Amos."

Graham promptly asked, "What's Amos about?"

I received a few shocked looks when I responded with, "I don't know. We'll find out tomorrow."

Maggie exclaimed loudly, "Didn't your mother read Amos to you?" I explained that my mother had not read Amos to me, so we would discover Amos together.

Of course I hold no grudge against my mom for not having read Amos to me. (Honestly, Mom!) My point is that Maggie thought our breakfast Bible reading was the norm. She thought everyone did this. Recently Maggie told me that the day just wouldn't seem right if we didn't read the Bible. That's exactly what I want! I spent years struggling with the discipline of reading God's Word, and I don't want my children to face this same struggle. I want Bible reading to be a natural part of their day, so much so that the day doesn't feel right unless they spend time in God's Word.

However, as much as I want Bible reading to be a habit for my children, I don't want it to be just a habit. I want them to get to know God through His Word. I want them to see Jesus and the gospel in our reading. I want them to delight in God's Word and delight in God Himself. By God's grace, I have seen this happening.

The morning we reached Psalm 52, I began by reading the heading in my Bible: "For the choir director. A Maskil of David, when Doeg the Edomite came and told Saul and said to him, 'David has come to the house of Ahimelech.'"

I checked the cross-reference and told the kids that this psalm was written by David in response to events we had read about in 1 Samuel. Psalm 52 consists of only nine verses, so we were finished quickly. When we finished the psalm, Graham asked if we could go back and reread what had happened in 1 Samuel. So we looked it up.

David was on the run from Saul and had gone to Ahimelech the priest. Ahimelech prayed for him and gave him the bread from the tabernacle and Goliath's sword. Doeg, one of Saul's men, had seen David with Ahimelech and went back to report the news to Saul. When he heard the news, Saul called for Ahimelech and the other priests of Nob. Saul was angry with Ahimelech for his apparent attempt to help David. Ultimately, Saul had all the priests killed, and then the entire city of Nob was put to the sword.

Boys love these action-packed passages, and this one only kindled Graham's appetite for more. He quickly asked if we could keep reading. The other children seemed to be attentive so I proceeded to the next chapter, in which David battles the Philistines. The moment I read the final words of that story, Graham was asking, "Can we read more?"

So I read how David met with

 **I KNEW THE** children were hiding truths about God's character in their hearts.

Jonathan and how Saul pursued David in the wilderness. The others were following along, and Graham was still eager for more. So I went on to the story of David hiding in the cave and cutting off a piece of Saul's robe. This was captivating for the older two, and I was managing to keep Benjamin and Emma involved, too.

When I finished reading the conversation between David and Saul, Graham wasted no time in begging, "Read more, read more." On we went! We read of Nabal and Abigail. When I reached the part where David takes Abigail as his wife, I was persuaded once again to keep reading. This time David spared Saul's life when he came upon Saul sleeping, and then David fled to the land of the Philistines. By the time we had heard of Saul consulting with the woman who was a spirit medium and Saul's conversation with Samuel, Benjamin and Emma were children who were naturally getting restless. That's when I glanced up at the clock. To my surprise, it was eleven o'clock. What started out as breakfast reading was leading into lunchtime!

Emma, who had been happy for most of this reading, was ready to revolt. You would be too if you were sitting in a high chair! I had been putting food and toys on her tray and giving her an occasional pat to keep her happy, but now her appetite was gone and so was her patience. I turned to Graham and said, "It's eleven o'clock. We have to stop." Although he was disappointed, he understood that conditions were no longer favorable for reading. But before we left the table, he looked at me and asked, "Can we do this again someday?"

The children were delighting in exploring God's Word, and I knew they were hiding truths about God's character in their hearts.

On another morning we were reading in Micah. Something in that day's reading reminded the kids of Shadrach, Meshach, and Abednego. When we finished our reading in Micah, one after another, they asked if we could go back and read the ever-popular story of the fiery furnace.

We turned to Daniel and read how King Nebuchadnezzar had made a huge golden image and invited all sorts of leaders to come to the dedication ceremony. A herald proclaimed that when they heard the sound of many instruments and "all kinds of music," all who were present must fall down and worship the statue. Anyone who did not fall down would be thrown into a furnace of blazing fire. (Our adrenaline was pumping!)

Some men came forward and told the king that there were some Jews, namely, Shadrach, Meshach, and Abednego, who refused to fall down and worship the effigy. The king was mad! In "rage and anger" he ordered these treasonous men to be brought to him. He asked them if what he had heard was true. Then the king said to them,

"Now if you are ready, at the moment you hear the sound of the horn, flute, lyre, trigon, psaltery and bagpipe and all kinds of music, to fall down and worship the image that I have made, very well. But if you do not worship, you will immediately be cast into the midst of a furnace of blazing fire; and what god is there who can deliver you out of my hands?" (Daniel 3:15)

When little Emma heard that question, "What god is there who can deliver you out of my hands?" she instantly cried out, "Jesus!"—much to the delight of her brothers and sister. Of course she was right! Jesus did deliver them out of the hands of the king and his fiery furnace.

I want my children to form the habit of reading the Bible. If they haven't spent time in God's Word, I want it to seem as if there's something not right about the day. But even more important, I want them to treasure God's Word.

I want them to be able to say with the psalmist, "How sweet are Your words to my taste! Yes, sweeter than honey to my mouth!" (Psalm 119:103). I want them to have those moments when they lose track of time as they delight in God's Word—and lose track of time as they marvel and delight in God Himself. I want them to read the Word of God and in a loud voice shout "Yay!" And I want them to confidently proclaim that the reason for that "yay"—in all of Scripture—is Jesus.

As they marvel and delight in God, my children will calibrate their hearts to His ways and long to please the One they love. In this way, their delight in God's Word (the law of the Lord) will shape their attitudes and actions.

DELIGHT BECOMES OBEDIENCE

Give me understanding, that I may observe Your law
and keep it with all my heart.
Make me walk in the path of Your commandments,
for I delight in it. Psalm 119:34–35

Wes and I tend to be relaxed, easygoing people, and our household operates in that same style. We find that mornings are plenty full just meeting the immediate needs of our children and getting Wes out the door. So the kids and I usually eat breakfast after Wes leaves for work. This means that Dad is rarely home for our morning Bible reading.

Wes has his own time of personal Bible study and

prayer, but he is also actively leading us as a family. In the evenings, he may read Scripture to us or share a time of prayer with us, play songs for us, show us a sermon he found online, or take us back over what we read that day. All the while he is directing our attention to Jesus and the gospel and applying God's Word to our family.

While these focused times together are extremely important, I think the most crucial thing Wes does to point us to Christ is just to spend a lot of time with us, both individually and as a family. He gets to know our hearts, and we get to know his. We know without a doubt that Wes loves Jesus because his life tells us.

So even though Wes is not with us as we read that one chapter each morning, he is guiding this undertaking of teaching our children the Word of God. So it makes sense that he keeps close track of where we are in our reading. Not long before we started in Genesis, our church gave us a copy of Robert Murray McCheyne's plan for reading through the Bible. I posted this plan on the front of our refrigerator, and after each day's reading I would circle the chapter we had completed. We weren't following the exact McCheyne plan, but it was a visible way to track our progress and an ideal way for Wes to check in and see where we were.

Many days the kids couldn't wait for their dad to get

home so they could tell him what we had read. Sometimes I couldn't wait either, and I would email him with a story of what had happened over breakfast.

I am grateful that Wes desires to point his family to God, and I lean heavily on his wisdom when issues arise as a result of our reading—like the time Graham seemed fixated on the idea of fasting.

One morning Wes was packing to leave on a business trip, when Graham announced, "While Dad is away, we should fast from sinning."

Wes and I were not really fully awake yet, and we both had the same response, "Fast from what?"

"Fast from sinning!" Graham said enthusiastically.

Oh, but he didn't stop there. Graham glanced at me and said, "*You* should do this, too, Mom." I felt more than a little self-conscious, but I had to admit that not sinning was a good idea. Wes voiced his support and gave me a big grin. After all, he was going to be out of town.

Then Graham's plan kicked into high gear. He smiled and said, "The reward for not sinning is doughnuts."

So I agreed that while Wes was away we would all "step up" our efforts not to sin. Wes promised to do his best not to sin during his trip, but he was particularly anxious to see how things would turn out on our end.

Of course we could hardly achieve a "total" fast from sinning during those few days that Wes was away, but we did our best and, in the end, we enjoyed the doughnuts.

Soon the subject of fasting came up again. We were sitting down to breakfast when Graham said, "I want to fast and pray that I will lose my tooth." He had a loose tooth that had been making it difficult for him to eat for a couple of weeks. Despite the attempts of Graham and Wes to pull it, the tooth was hanging on. So Graham decided the time had come to fast and pray. He was serious. He was ready to skip lunch and start immediately.

I wasn't sure how to respond, so I put him off until I could slip away and call Wes. "Help! Graham wants to fast and pray that he'll lose his tooth, and he wants to start now. What do I do?" Wes coached me through some ways to talk with Graham. He wanted Graham to have a firm grip on why Christians fast and he also wanted to encourage Graham's positive desire to seek God's help. Graham and I talked but, in the end, he decided to think and learn more about fasting and concentrate on praying about his tooth.

Within a few days, fasting was in Graham's conversation again. This time he really took me by surprise. He declared, "I want to fast and pray that I will see Jesus return." Honestly, I don't think this idea had ever crossed *my* mind.

I was eager for Wes to come home that evening so I could tell him of this awesome statement his son had

I COULD NEVER write a book telling how to teach children to want to fast and pray—because I didn't want to fast and pray myself!

made, but Graham beat me to it. Not long after Wes arrived, Graham shared with him that he wanted to fast and pray that he would see Jesus return. Wes quickly responded, "I'm really glad that you want to fast and pray that you will see Jesus return, but, Graham, are *you* ready for Jesus to return?" Now I was not only amazed by what Graham had said but astonished over my husband's response. *That* idea had not crossed my mind either.

Not long after these events, Wes and I were having dinner with a friend and were relating how Graham had suddenly become interested in fasting and praying. Our friend exclaimed, "If you could write a book that told parents how to teach their children to *want* to fast and pray, you could sell 100,000 copies." We laughed and went on with our conversation. But later it occurred to me that I could never write a book that would tell parents how to teach their children to want to fast and pray—because I didn't want to fast and pray myself! Graham's desire to fast and pray wasn't inherited from his parents, or learned from our example. Graham got this desire from God. Graham had heard stories in the Old Testament of people who fasted and prayed, and he wanted to participate. He wanted to obey. Graham's desire was prompted by the Word of God.

By the way, sometime later Graham did participate in this discipline. He fasted from sweets for an entire month and prayed for the salvation of a family member. Wes, Maggie, and I joined him, but he was the one who initiated the fast. It was an inspiring and humbling month for his parents.

FROM THE PAGES OF GOD'S WORD
INTO OUR EVERYDAY LIVES

Oh, that my ways may be established
to keep Your statutes! Psalm 119:5

As we expose our children to God's Word, we count on God's promise that His Word "will not return to Me empty, without accomplishing what I desire" (Isaiah 55:11). We pray that God will tune Graham's and Maggie's and Benjamin's and Emma's hearts to love Him and to desire to obey Him. We've seen our children learn from God's Word in ways we could never have anticipated, and our faith has grown right along with theirs.

When the Going Gets Tough: How We Get through the Hard Passages

4

> All Scripture is inspired by God and profitable for teaching, for reproof, for correction, for training in righteousness.
> 2 Timothy 3:16

*I*f you are at all familiar with God's Word, you can imagine that there were plenty of days when I dashed off to make furtive phone calls to Wes at work, "How on earth am I supposed to explain—?" Fill in the blank: why the patriarchs had multiple wives, what circumcision is all about, why bears came along to eat up guys who teased a prophet because he was bald, whatever! Reading God's Word with children necessarily entails encountering some accounts that read like they ought to come with a PG-13 rating and passages that are tough even for grown-ups to encounter and absorb.

Mostly, the children and I tackled them, large and small, easy and hard, with varying success in understanding and application. But we moved ahead in confidence that all of God's Word is "profitable" for training in righteousness. And we found that the promise of Hebrews 4:12 is true: the Word of God *is* living and active, sometimes especially when it's hard for us to read or hear.

Our family especially encountered challenges in Job, Isaiah, and Leviticus.

UNDERSTANDING JOB

The Lord gave and the Lord has taken away.
Blessed be the name of the Lord. Job 1:21

After a little more than two years of reading the Bible, the children and I arrived at the book of Job. When I say that Job was difficult, that might be an understatement. Job can be a hard book for adults to sift through, but reading this book to children was especially tough.

The book begins by describing Job's remarkable wealth and his righteous character. Then suddenly we are transported to a scene in heaven and told of a significant conversation between the Lord and Satan. (A conversation not revealed to Job, by the way.) Satan is, at that point, allowed to test Job, and in this testing Job loses virtually all that he has. The first chapter concludes with Job's amazing response to his situation.

Then we come to chapter 2, where God allows Satan to test Job still further by attacking his health. When Job's friends hear of all Job's adversity, the Bible says, "They made an appointment to come together to sympathize with him and comfort him." When they arrive, they are so grieved by Job's appearance that they take on the posture of mourning and sit with him on the ground for seven days and nights without saying a word.

So far it's a riveting story, right? These first two chapters are completely captivating — the kind of reading that keeps you on the edge of your seat and wanting more.

Sure, but then comes thirty-five chapters (count 'em: *thirty-five!*) of extensive, *extensive* diatribes as Job and his friends discuss and discuss and *discuss* Job's circumstances. Without a doubt, God gave us these thirty-five chapters, and there is much to be learned from this discussion. However, reading and searching for understanding of these chapters with small children can be incredibly arduous. Not too far into these thirty-five chapters, my daughter Maggie sighed and said, "Can we *please* read something else? He keeps saying the same thing over and over again."

In an effort to keep my children's attention and encourage them to press on, I began to tell them, "God is going to speak. Soon God is going to speak." Of course, I started saying this about chapter 10. When does He finally speak? God speaks in chapter 38. Day after day, I would proclaim again, "Hang in there just a little while longer. God is going to speak."

Then the day finally came when God was going to speak. We had, at long last, reached chapter 38. My children were mesmerized. They, along with Job, had been waiting for what seemed like *forever* for God to have His say, and now it was finally going to happen. I began with "Today is the day that God speaks." There was complete silence. I actually had their undivided attention. Then I read the Lord's answer to Job. All eyes were fixed on me as I read:

> Then the Lord answered Job out of the whirlwind and said, "Who is this that darkens counsel by words without knowledge? Now gird up your loins like a man, and I will ask you, and you instruct Me! . . . "Where were you when I laid the foundation of the earth? . . .
>
> "Have you ever in your life commanded the morning, and caused the dawn to know its place? . . .
>
> "Have you entered into the springs of the sea or walked in the recesses of the deep? . . .
>
> "Have you entered the storehouses of the snow, or have you seen the storehouses of the hail?"

I was about two-thirds into the chapter when Benjamin, only two-and-a-half, quietly asked, "Can we sing 'He's Got the Whole World in His Hands'?"

For a moment I was speechless. Like a typical mom, I was about to cry. In his childlike way, he understood the passage! He understood that God does have the whole world in His hands, even Job with all his trouble.

We did sing. We sang again and again. I don't think I've ever sung "He's Got the Whole World in His Hands" with such emotion. At the end of the singing, Benjamin got a big hug and a kiss.

After that memorable day, I developed a great fondness for the book of Job. Little did I know how soon God would use the book of Job again in our lives. About a year later, I was pregnant with our fifth child. I announced the news to my husband by shoveling a huge "5" in the snow in our backyard. We were all extremely excited. Unfortunately, at only ten and a half weeks, I miscarried. The loss of this little life left me physically and emotionally weak. It also left me contemplating life and God's plans. I had questions, and I was on a search for answers. But life went on.

Six months later, I was in the doctor's office, driven there by pain from a kidney stone. After some testing, I learned that not only did I have a kidney stone but I was also going to have another baby. Once the pain of the kidney stone abated, I was filled with anticipation once more.

This time we suffered the miscarriage at nine weeks. Wes was with me at the ultrasound that confirmed this loss. When we walked away, I had no desire to ask deep questions or search for answers. I was numb. Honestly, I wanted to stay numb. I didn't really want to do anything, but the thing I dreaded the most was telling our children of another loss.

Our children had been understandably naive about the first miscarriage. They were young and didn't comprehend what was happening. But, as Wes and I had processed the loss of that baby, the children began to gain a greater understanding. I knew the loss of this second baby would have a different effect on them. I was not ready to face that.

When we came home from the doctor, we quietly shared this news with our friends who had been watching the kids. Once they left, it was time to turn our attention to our playful, enthusiastic children. Eventually Wes found a quiet moment and called us all into the living room. I sat on the couch, not really wanting to walk through this again myself—much less with them.

Wes told the kids that he wanted to read something to us first. He opened his Bible and began reading Job. He read about the tragedy that had befallen Job, and then he read Job's response in Job 1:21:

> Then Job arose and tore his robe and shaved his head, and he fell to the ground and worshiped. He said, "Naked I came from my mother's womb, and naked I shall return there. The Lord gave and the Lord has taken away. Blessed be the name of the Lord."

Wes gently told the kids that we had lost another baby. He shared with them his own pain over this loss, and then he led us in prayer. I did not yet want to pray. I just couldn't get those Job-like words out of my mouth. I had never felt more like the weaker vessel. I can't tell you exactly what Wes prayed, but I can tell you he worshipped God. It was as though Wes was standing before God on behalf of the family, saying what I could not say and what our children didn't know how to say.

Our children knew the story of Job because we had read it a year before. They knew what had happened to him and how he responded. Now they were being taught how to apply it to their own lives, and I was being reminded of how to apply it to mine.

God has taught me much about worship and His sovereignty through the life of Job. As difficult as Job can be for me, I look forward to reading it again.

AFTER DARK DAYS, SALVATION!

And [God] will send them a Savior and a Champion,
and He will deliver them. Isaiah 19:20

When the children and I got to the book of Isaiah, we felt we had entered rough waters. I take some comfort in knowing that many readers have a tough time under- standing what Isaiah is saying. While there are wonder- ful prophetic passages about Christ in Isaiah, the long passages about rebellion, judgment, and devastation had taken a toll. Isaiah had been thorny; the reading was hav- ing a somber effect on us.

Then came the morning we read Isaiah 19, a message to Egypt. At first the verses carried the familiar tone of other passages about the just wrath of God. We read about the Lord riding on a swift cloud and that He is about to come to Egypt. When He comes, even the idols will tremble and the hearts of the Egyptians will melt within them. They will fight with one another, and they will be delivered into the hands of a cruel master.

We read that the seas and the rivers will dry up. There will be no fish for the fishermen. The fields will dry up and the land beside the Nile will be parched. The workers and the weavers will be in despair. In the midst of this, the counsel of the wisest of Pharaoh's advisers would become stupid. Then the passage describes how the princes and those who were the cornerstones of her tribes have "led Egypt astray." We read that, in that day, the Egyptians "will tremble and be in dread because of the waving of the hand of the Lord of hosts." It was bad news, and bad news, and *more bad news* for Egypt.

There was not a happy mood at the breakfast table as I read. My children were serious and quiet. But I didn't really realize how attentively they were listening or the full effect this passage was having on them until I read the following:

> In that day there will be an altar to the Lord in the midst of the land of Egypt, and a pillar to the Lord near its border. It will become a sign and a witness to the Lord of hosts in the land of Egypt; for they will cry to the Lord because of oppressors, and **He will send them a Savior and a Champion, and He will deliver them**. (Isaiah 19:19–20)

Suddenly, without any notice, my older son jumped up in his chair and shouted in a loud voice, "Yay!" Salvation was coming, and he was so relieved and happy to hear it, he just couldn't hold it in. He had to shout for joy.

Virtually, but also in real time, my children were experiencing what it feels like to wait for the Lord to act, and then to rejoice in God's deliverance.

It made me want to shout for joy!

UH-OH! LEVITICUS!

For the word of God is living and active and sharper than any two-edged sword. Hebrews 4:12

Picture us gathered around the table, way back near the beginning, enjoying the dramatic stories of the patriarchs all through Genesis, and the amazing stories of Moses and Joshua in Exodus, when it dawns on me what is coming next: Leviticus. The thought gave me a chill.

I had never read the entire Bible, and I had certainly never tackled reading Leviticus by myself. The idea of reading "the law" to my children (at that time, four years of age and under) was not the least bit appealing. So when we reached Leviticus, I did the only thing I knew to do: I skipped it.

Though skipping the book seemed like the logical thing to do at the time, the knowledge that I had not read Leviticus bothered me. The further we got into the Bible, the more I was reminded that we had passed over an entire book. There were some other short passages that I had not read to our children, or I had summarized, but this was the only complete book we had not read. This thought nagged at me.

I GOT INTO the habit of reading in a commentary about the background and setting of a book.

However, even though I wanted to read the entire Bible, I didn't know exactly how and where to squeeze in Leviticus discreetly. So I pushed the problem onto a back burner and left it alone.

Now jump ahead with me. We made it all the way to the New Testament. When we started reading through the Epistles (letters to the new believers), I needed a bit of assistance. So I got into the habit of reading in a commentary about the background and setting of a book before we began to read it. I found this to be immensely helpful in giving my children, and me, a better understanding of the context in which each letter was written, thereby helping us understand what was being said.

Eventually we came to the book of Hebrews. That morning I picked up the *MacArthur Bible Commentary* and checked out what he had to say about Hebrews. There I was, reading along, when one statement leaped off the page at me. (Well, that's how it felt anyway.) John MacArthur said, "In order to have an understanding of Hebrews, it is essential to have an understanding of Leviticus." Uh-oh, Leviticus! There it was, the one book we had skipped. What was I going to do?

GRAHAM WAS appalled. I had passed over a book of the Bible. He kept repeating, "I can't believe you skipped something."

I said to my four children, "Dr. MacArthur just said that in order to understand Hebrews, you need to understand Leviticus. Well . . . we never read Leviticus. I skipped it."

You would have thought I had confessed some horrible atrocity. My older son—nine by now—looked at me in shock and said, "You skipped something?" Graham was appalled. I had passed over a book of the Bible! How could I do such a thing? He wouldn't let up. He kept repeating, "I can't believe you skipped something."

I tried to explain that he was only about four years old at the time and that Leviticus is really hard, but that didn't seem to matter. I had let him down. This was big.

So I told him and the other three, who were much less opinionated on the topic, "Well, now is our chance. If we need to understand Leviticus in order to understand Hebrews, then let's go back and read it now. What do you say? Raise your hand if you want to read Leviticus now."

Let me just slip in a word of advice for you: it is never a good idea to put these things to a vote. I mean, what did

I expect? What I got was a split decision, two in favor and two opposed. So, like any good leader, I cast the deciding vote. And we went back and read Leviticus.

Now this does not mean that "the law" was easy for us. It is tough reading. I got a lot of "gross," "yuck," and "huh?" during that reading. But we made it. We read Leviticus, and then we read Hebrews. And John MacArthur was right. Even with our limited knowledge of the law, knowing about the law helped us have a greater understanding of, and appreciation for, the sacrifice of Jesus on behalf of sinners.

There was a place to squeeze in Leviticus, after all.

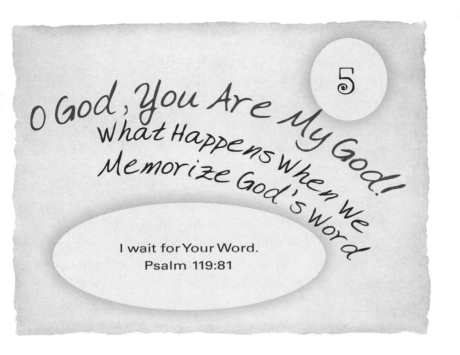

O God, You Are My God!
What Happens When We Memorize God's Word

> I wait for Your Word.
> Psalm 119:81

One evening Wes came home from work and quickly relayed to me a conversation he had with a friend of ours. He said, "I was sitting in my office and she was standing on the other side of my desk, shaking her bony little finger in my face and saying, 'You need to get those kids to memorize Scripture.'" I knew that our friend did not have "bony fingers" and I had my doubts that she was shaking said bony finger in his face, but I did not doubt that she had made the statement. And I was confident she had made it with some intensity.

However, as Wes reported the conversation, it felt as though he was waving *his* "bony finger" in my face and

saying, "You need to get those kids to memorize Scripture."
My initial reaction was, "How do I do that? When do I do
that? I've taken on the job of reading the entire Bible to
them, which is going to take *eight years.* How can I take
on one more thing?" Of course, I didn't actually verbalize
these thoughts, but I was certain they were written all
over my face.

Over the next few days, Wes's words and the words of
our friend began to sink in. They were right; we did need
to memorize more of God's Word. And although the kids
had just started attending an Awana program, which was
wonderful at getting us started in memorizing
Scripture, I knew that we needed to get
even more of the Bible into our memories. Yet I really hadn't a clue where to
start. I wasn't sure when we could do it
or how much the kids could take in.
One morning as we were reading
the Bible at breakfast, I realized
that the Bible reading was working pretty well. We had found
a groove of sorts. I had them all
in one place at one time, and
they were attentive, for the most part. So
I thought perhaps we could memorize at lunch. We
would all be together and sitting still. I decided to give
it a try.

I was feeling ambitious and determined, in that high

mood, that we should memorize entire chapters instead of single verses. For our first passage I selected Psalm 121: *"I will lift up my eyes to the mountain; from where shall my help come? My help comes from the Lord, who made heaven and earth . . ."*

It's a great psalm, and each child enjoyed it.

So at breakfast time I tried to keep their mouths full so they wouldn't talk while I was reading Scripture, and at lunch I would tell them, "Hurry up and chew and swallow so you can say your verse." We would say one verse for several days until we had it down, and then we'd add the next verse to it. We would say the passage together and then take turns saying it individually. (They would guess a number behind my back to see who would get to go next.) Memorizing was actually turning out to be fun, and they were soaking it in like little sponges. And I was keeping up, too.

The breakfast reading and lunchtime memorizing became our pattern. Before long we had memorized several psalms and the Lord's Prayer. And each time we reached a new verse, it seemed as though God was helping us along. We would hear the new verse quoted all throughout the week. Our pastor would be preaching and quote the exact verse we were working on. We would be in conversation when someone would mention "our verse." God was graciously rehearsing with us.

 **OUT OF THE** mouth of this babe came the praise of God from the Word of God.

We had been "getting those kids to memorize Scripture" for a couple of years, when one night Wes came home feeling troubled. He had sensed an overwhelming burden to pray for the salvation of our children. That morning at work he had heard a testimony regarding salvation, and the need to pray for the souls of our children had been weighing heavy on him the rest of the day. Later that night Wes told me more details of the story he'd heard, and we prayed for our kids and went to bed. At that moment, I was not really sharing his intense feelings, but sometime during the night, this burden spread from his side of the bed to mine. By the time I got up the next morning, the concern for our children was resting heavily on me as well.

When the kids and I sat down to breakfast, I started to pray. My breakfast prayer quickly turned into pleading for the salvation of our children, with our children listening ever so quietly. My prayer went rather long. By the time I was done, I was certain they were wondering, *What's up with Mom?*

But of course I couldn't stop there. When the praying ended, I suddenly became an evangelist and the "beseeching" set in. We had been reading through Jeremiah, and I began telling the kids how Jeremiah had been preaching repentance for years but the people would not listen. I told them how they needed to realize they were sinners in need of a Savior. They needed to repent and put their trust in Jesus.

I was exceptionally long-winded in my plea, and my little people were wide-eyed over Mom's intense start to the day. I was still making my somber appeal when Benjamin, four at the time, said something. I wasn't sure what he said, but I knew the word *God* had come out of his mouth. So I asked him to repeat what he said. He did, but unfortunately I couldn't understand any more than I had the first time. My daughter Maggie acted as interpreter: "He's trying to say our verse."

We had been memorizing Psalm 63 and Benjamin was trying to quote it to me. So I asked him if he would like for me to say it with him. And we began:

O God, You are my God; I shall seek You earnestly;
My soul thirsts for You, my flesh yearns for You,
in a dry and weary land where there is no water.
Thus I have seen You in the sanctuary,
to see Your power and Your glory.
Because Your lovingkindness is better than life,
my lips will praise You.

By this time my voice was quivering, my eyes were welling with tears, and I was having a difficult time getting the words out. I stopped because those were the verses we knew well. We had been working on the next verse, but I didn't think he would know it. However, as soon as I stopped, Benjamin said, "No, I want to say the whole thing." So we went on.

> So I will bless You as long as I live;
> I will lift up my hands in Your name.

In the middle of my appeal for their repentance and salvation, God had prompted this little boy to quote Scripture to his mother. Out of the mouth of this babe came the praise of God from the Word of God. And a renewed trust in God came to his mother. It's an amazing thing to plead with your children about their relationship with God and have a child respond by quoting Scripture—and quoting a Scripture that claims God as his own and commits to bless the Lord through all of his life.

"O God, You are my God." Lord, let that be the cry of all my children's hearts as long as they live!

Sovereign Timing:
How God Continually Orchestrated Our Reading

6

But he who boasts is to
boast in the Lord.
2 Corinthians 10:17

During our reading of the Bible, I have often been amazed by God's perfect timing. Unfortunately, sometimes it takes me awhile to recognize His sovereign and active hand in our lives. As John Piper puts it, "In every situation, God is always doing a thousand different things you cannot see and you do not know."

One evening while we were eating dinner, the phone rang. Wes answered the phone and whispered to me who was on the other end. As he talked, I had a sense of what the conversation was about. I have a talent for figuring out an entire conversation by listening only to one side— or at least I presume I have figured it out.

 **WES AND I** were both sensing that we should try living with one car for a while.

This time my perceptions were correct. Our friends were having car trouble and wanted to borrow one of our cars. Wes hung up the phone, he filled in the missing details, and we agreed to help our friends.

Our main mode of transportation was a Chrysler minivan, but we also owned a ten-year-old Suburban that Wes drove to work. At that time, our friends had a houseful of teenagers who needed to go in different directions. They wondered if we could spare our Suburban until their car situation was fixed. So the next day Wes took them "the Vehicle," as we affectionately referred to it.

A few days passed. We were pleasantly surprised at how smoothly our lives were going with only one car. It took a bit more advanced planning, but for our stage of life, one car was entirely doable. Amazingly—and I believe this was entirely God's work—within a few days Wes and I were both sensing that we should try living with one car for a while. The Vehicle was paid for, and we were both feeling prompted to give it away.

Our friends were still borrowing the Suburban, but they already had a plan under way to replace their car. So we started looking around for someone else who might need this transportation more than we did. The next Sunday as we were leaving church, Wes mentioned some friends of ours and asked, "I wonder if they could use a car?" Four of their five children were high school and college age, so my response was, "I'm sure they could *always* use a car."

We drove out of the church parking lot, and the conversation quickly moved on to lunch and our afternoon plans. We didn't mention the car again until we were on our way back that night. As we sat at a stoplight just around the corner from church, I glanced across the street and saw the very same couple Wes had mentioned that morning. They were walking through a used-car lot! Wes and I looked at each other and laughed. We had our answer.

After the service ended that night, Wes talked to these friends about the Suburban, assuring them that we had been praying about giving it away and now believed that God wanted us to give it to them. Wes told them that the Suburban was on loan to someone else, but as soon as it was returned to us, we would arrange a day to give it to them.

In just a few days, our other friends returned the Vehicle to us. When I looked inside, I was embarrassed that we had given it to them in such a mess. There was a considerable amount of miscellaneous "stuff" in the back, and the Suburban was in dire need of a good cleaning. We couldn't possibly hand it over looking like this. Wes agreed and mentioned that he wanted to repair the spare tire and have the oil changed. So he told the soon-to-be new owners that, after we gave the Vehicle a good once-over, we would set a date to give it to them.

It turned out to be an extremely busy week for Wes at work. He needed to stay late for several nights. By the time he came home at the end of late nights in the office, he and I were just plain exhausted. Cleaning the Vehicle completely slipped our minds. An entire week went by.

Wes called me from work one day, feeling a pang of guilt, and said, "We have got to clean the Suburban." He wanted to keep his word in a timely manner. We agreed to set a date to give this family the car, and we would somehow get it clean before that day came. Wes started driving the minivan to work, and the kids and I began the work of cleaning. Over the weekend Wes took care of the mechanical aspects. We ran it through a car wash, and we were ready to go—or so we thought.

The date had been set for Tuesday, but when Monday arrived I was reminded of one small detail we had been putting off. We had not told the kids we were giving away the Vehicle. They knew we were working really hard to get it clean, but they didn't know why. They were sure to be upset if they were not given a chance to give it a proper good-bye. (We have some sentimental kids.) Reluctantly I called Wes and said, "Do you think we could delay this one more time? We really need to tell the kids." He, too, had been unsure how to break the news and agreed that our kids needed a little time to adjust, so he delayed the transaction a couple of days. We planned to tell the children that night.

That night came—and went. And guess what? *We forgot to tell them!* It never crossed our minds. The next morning I was out for a walk when it hit me: I'm going to have to tell the kids by myself—*today*. I was thinking intently about how to break the news, when I remembered what we had read the morning before. The kids and I had been reading 2 Corinthians 8, where Paul urges the Corinthian church to follow through on a gift they had promised. It was the perfect way to tell the kids about giving away the Suburban. Let me add, although I have heard many sermons from Corinthians, I was quite a novice at reading this part of Scripture. So, honestly, I had no idea what we were about to read that morning.

I got back from my walk, and Wes dashed off to work. Soon the kids and I sat down to breakfast. I reminded them of what we had read the morning before—how Paul was urging the Corinthians to give as they had promised and encouraging them to prove their love for the saints by giving out of their abundance.

Then I gave them the news that Dad and I had felt God prompting us to give away "the Vehicle," and we wanted to obey. I told them that because it was paid for, we had the freedom to give it away. Then I said we had already found a special family who would give it a perfect home. This was a great opportunity for us to exercise this "act of grace," as Paul called it.

They asked a lot of questions, and there was much discussion regarding the details. Then we turned our attention to our Bible reading for the day: 2 Corinthians 9. That morning I could have simply said, "Your dad and I feel God prompting us to give away the Vehicle," and that would have been fine. But God had much more planned for us. As we walked through the day's reading, God, through His Word, explained to the kids—and reminded me—how and why we give.

> Now this I say, he who sows sparingly will also reap sparingly, and he who sows bountifully will also reap bountifully. (2 Corinthians 9:6)

I shared with our children that we had something significant to give and had an opportunity to give it. I said, "We will reap bountifully if we give bountifully. We will not necessarily reap materially but spiritually."

> Each one must do just as he has purposed in his heart, not grudgingly or under compulsion, for God loves a cheerful giver. (2 Corinthians 9:7)

"God made it clear that He wants us to give. We do it gladly, with no hesitation. We're not giving because someone is forcing us to give or making us feel guilty if we don't. We want to give."

> And God is able to make all grace abound to you, so that always having all sufficiency in everything, you may have an abundance for every good deed; as it is written, "He scattered abroad, He gave to the poor, His righteousness endures forever." Now He who supplies seed to the sower and bread for food will supply and multiply your seed for sowing and increase the harvest of your righteousness; you will be enriched in everything for all liberality. (2 Corinthians 9:8–11)

"God will give the grace we need to let go of the Vehicle. He hasn't asked us to give it away without giving us the ability to do without it. Our friends have a need that we have been given—by God—the ability to meet."

... which through us is producing thanksgiving to God. For the ministry of this service is not only fully supplying the needs of the saints, but is also overflowing through many thanksgivings to God. Because of the proof given by this ministry, they will glorify God for your obedience to your confession of the gospel of Christ, and for the liberality of your contribution to them and to all. (2 Corinthians 9:11–13)

"We're not giving so our friends can thank us or pat us on the back. But our giving will cause them to thank God. They will glorify God because He met their need in an unexpected way and will thank Him because of it."

... while they also, by prayer on your behalf, yearn for you because of the surpassing grace of God in you. (2 Corinthians 9:14)

"And if our friends thanking God is not awesome enough, get this: they may pray for us because of our gift to them. That's amazing!"

> Thanks be to God for His indescribable gift!
> (2 Corinthians 9:15)

"After all, God has given us the greatest gift of all—His Son!"

The *exact* morning we got around to telling our children we were giving away something we treasured, God had planned to teach us how to give through that day's chapter. Second Timothy 3:16–17 says, "All Scripture is inspired by God and profitable for teaching, for reproof, for correction, for training in righteousness; so that the man of God may be adequate, equipped for every good work." That morning God used His Word to equip us—make us ready—for this good work.

It wasn't until a week or so later that I realized just how amazing this event actually was. God knew our friends' car would break down. He knew He would prompt us to realize we could go without the Vehicle and meet a need. He even knew that we would neglect cleaning it for a week! He knew we would delay giving it away (again!) in order to tell our children. He knew we would forget to tell our children! He knew when we would read 2 Corinthians 8. God knew that on the morning our children heard the news of the Vehicle, we would be reading 2 Corinthians 9. The Lord didn't just know about these events, His sovereign hand guided them all.

O Lord, You have searched me and known me!
You know when I sit down and when I rise up;
You understand my thought from afar.
You scrutinize my path and my lying down,
and are intimately acquainted with all my ways.
Even before there is a word on my tongue,
behold, O Lord, you know it all.
You have enclosed me behind and before,
and laid Your hand upon me.
Such knowledge is too wonderful for me;
it is too high, I cannot attain to it. (Psalm 139:1–6)

We Did It!
You Can, Too

> Blessed is he who reads and those
> who hear the words of the prophecy.
> Revelation 1:3

*T*he kids and I normally read from God's Word at
breakfast, so Saturday night was not a typical time
for us to read. But one Saturday night Wes was out of
town, and I was looking for a pre-bedtime activity. And
we were about to start Revelation. I was nervously excited
to get underway.

I had been diving into a commentary by John
MacArthur for some background and setting information before tackling Revelation, a book of prophecy that
had always seemed difficult and intimidating. I was encouraged by Dr. MacArthur's assertion that "Revelation is
the greatest book ever written." I reported this opinion to

the kids, and MacArthur's words made us all the more eager to get started.

Having gotten a sense of the backdrop for this book, the five of us snuggled up on the couch and I began to read Revelation. Chapter 1 was enthralling. The launching of John's vision was reminiscent of Ezekiel's, except this time none of my children thought it was weird. They were all silent and wide-eyed with amazement.

When we finished the first chapter, the kids wanted more. They were energized and enthusiastic, and so was I. What was Christ going to say to these churches? So we read chapter 2—and it fell completely flat. I didn't understand. The children didn't understand. We were lost. What had Christ just said to these churches? We hadn't a clue. My children went to bed confused, and I went to bed thinking Revelation was going to kill us.

I figured I had until Monday morning to get some answers. Wes was still out of town, and our phone calls were too short to fully convey the depth of my concern over our reading. On Sunday I pulled out all the commentaries we owned that discussed Revelation and began digging for the meaning of chapter 2.

What I learned left me in awe, reminded once again that God's thoughts are higher than mine. While I'm certain I have not plumbed the depths of Christ's words to these churches, His words are nevertheless understandable. Christ used circumstances, economics, social structure, and even geography to convey His message unmistakably to each church.

When Wes came home Sunday evening, I told him about our venture into Revelation. I tapped into his wisdom as I processed my newfound information. I felt deeply grateful for the wisdom of the Christian writers who had helped clear my confusion, and I was thankful, too, for the wisdom of mature Christians around me.

On Monday morning, I read Revelation 2 again, explaining what I'd learned about the content and the context. This time my children were able to join me in marveling at the wisdom of God.

We visited those commentaries frequently and asked lots of questions during our reading of Revelation—a wonderful, mysterious, difficult, and sometimes alarming word that God has given. When we were about halfway through the book, my son Benjamin expressed his misgivings about John MacArthur's earlier comment. He looked at me and said, "Revelation is 'the best book ever written'? . . . Well . . . I don't know."

Revelation stimulated much discussion around our breakfast table and gave me ample opportunity to run to Wes with questions. Nevertheless, we forged ahead.

On March 19, 2007 (after only five years, not the estimated eight!), the kids and I completed our first reading of the entire Bible. I had counted ahead to the day we would finish so Wes and I could plan a day of celebration for our family.

Wes took the day off from work. He and I made a huge breakfast for the kids. We all took our places around the table. Wes prayed for us, and then I read the last three chapters of Revelation.

The week before, Wes and I had confiscated Graham's new Bible to have his name embossed on the front and to inscribe a dedication inside from Mom and Dad. We also bought new Bibles for Maggie, Benjamin, and Emma and wrote words of dedication in them. After I read the last words of Revelation, Wes presented each child with a Bible and read each inscription. Then Wes pulled out his own surprise— a new, leather-bound Bible for me! It was a moving moment, as he read the inscription. He congratulated me on my first complete reading of the Bible and thanked me for taking this journey with our children.

The rest of the day was spent just enjoying our time

GOD DID NOT open up His Word to us because of who we are. He spoke to us through His Word because of who He is.

together. We even threw in a trip to a local chocolate factory. Chocolate goes well with any celebration!

On that same day, our pastor, Brian, and his wife, Holly, were expecting their third child. Holly was scheduled to be induced that morning, so on our way to the chocolate factory, we stopped by the hospital and I ran up to see if their little girl had made her debut.

As I was searching for the right room, I ran into Brian in the hall. He wondered how I had managed to get to the hospital alone on a weekday, so I explained that Wes and the kids were in the car and we were out celebrating that we had finished reading the Bible.

Brian was aware of our journey through Scripture. He congratulated me, and then he said, "You are the only people I know who have read straight through the Bible with their children." Now Brian has pastored a couple of different churches and his father was a pastor, so he has been in the company of believers all his life. He said these words to encourage me, and his words did just that. However, while I felt elated over having read the entire Bible with my children, I also felt distressed that reading the entire Bible with kids was rare. After all, if I could do it, anybody could.

I'm that undisciplined person. I'm that slow reader who's not particularly dynamic or animated. And while I think my children are extraordinary, in reality they are probably not any more extraordinary than you think your children are. (Notice I said "probably.") And my husband, while he's my pillar, would openly tell you all his frailties. Our only "in" with God is Jesus Christ, just like yours.

So if we Wards are just an ordinary family, then God did not open up His Word to us because of who we are. He spoke to us through His Word because of who He is. If He wants to reveal Himself to *us* through His Word, then I earnestly believe that He wants to reveal Himself to *you* through His Word.

I am thrilled to declare what God has done in our family. I could shout from a mountaintop, "We read the Bible, and we heard from God!" But right after that, I would be compelled to shout even louder, "You can, too!"

Sweeter than Honey: Lessons I Learned

> For whatever was written in earlier times was written for our instruction, that through perseverance and the encouragement of the Scriptures we might have hope.
>
> **Romans 15:4**

*I*f I took the time to tell you all about the ways God worked in our lives as His Word soaked into us, day by day, this book would be too heavy to lift! But if you are on the brink of starting to read the Bible with your family, it might encourage you to know some of what I learned during the great adventure of reading through the whole of Scripture with my kids.

IT'S NOT ABOUT ME

I count all things to be loss in view of the
surpassing value of knowing Christ Jesus my Lord.
Philippians 3:8

When I was a second grader in Mrs. Fields's class, there was a large box located on a shelf next to the window. This was the "SRA Reading Lab." Each day as I sat in my place in the rows of little desks that faced Mrs. Fields, I would hear her encourage us to go to the box and select a book once we had finished our assignments. This was meant to be a treat, a bonus. For me, it was torture.

I RARELY ATTEMPTED reading for pleasure; for me, there was no pleasure in reading.

The SRA books were color coded. After a student read all the books in one color, she could advance to the next color, and on to the next and the next. But if I finished my work, I did everything possible to appear to be busy so that I did not have to go to the reading lab. I knew that as soon as I rose from my seat to go to the SRA box, every eye would be on me, and I would be humiliated in front of the entire class when the other students saw my color—the lowest reading level. The more I declined the opportunity to go and retrieve a book, the further behind I fell and the more embarrassed I became. I spent the second grade trying to avoid the SRA Reading Lab.

Fast-forward to my fifth-grade reading class. There I was, sitting in the back of a dark room facing one of those large projection screens on a three-legged stand. My technology-friendly teacher was way ahead of his time and was using a projector to improve the reading skills of his measly little fifth graders. He clicked on the projector, and a small rectangle of light appeared on the screen. Within the rectangle of light were about four words. Then he clicked another button and the words scrolled across this rectangle like the news scrolls across the bottom of CNN. Next, he intentionally turned it to the fastest setting to cause panic and screams of "No, please no" from the roomful of anxious ten-year-olds. Then he gradually decreased the speed until he had a collective "Okay" from the class. But he didn't get my okay. Inside I was yelling, "The words are still moving too fast!" but on the outside, I remained silent.

And so I grew up not liking to read. I read slowly, and it was frustrating and embarrassing. I rarely attempted reading for pleasure; for me, there was no pleasure in it.

I only read what I had to and never really enjoyed it. This feeling carried over into my attempts at Bible study. For years I was convinced that a good student of the Bible reads fast and in mass quantities. So when I tried to read the number of chapters I thought I "should" read, it took me forever. My attempts at Bible study were almost always short-lived, and they all ended the same—with me feeling like a failure.

My failed Bible-reading endeavors were all about one thing: me. I evaluated my speed, my volume, my understanding, and my talent (or lack of talent). Even when I wasn't discouraged by comparing myself to what I imagined other godly people accomplished, I let *my* schedule, *my* likes, and *my* dislikes dictate my time. The focus was on me. But by the time I began reading through the Bible with my children, it wasn't about me anymore. This time it was about God. I wanted to know God and impart that knowledge to my children. That single adjustment in my thinking completely changed the outcome.

God graciously turned my gaze to Him. Then He gave me the desire to read His Word with four tiny children. Reading to children gave me an "excuse" to slow down. It gave me a reason to tackle only short passages at a time. It felt acceptable to read only one chapter, which gave me time to meditate on what we'd read. I discovered that God is not concerned about speed-reading or how I measure up to other believers. God is looking at my heart. God has poured out grace upon grace and has adjusted my heart to desire to seek Him through His Word.

ACCOUNTABILITY IS A BLESSING

Therefore encourage one another and build
up one another, just as you also are doing.
1 Thessalonians 5:11

You may be familiar with the concept of an "accountability partner." Christians often pair up or get into a group to hold each other "accountable" to your shared goal of serving the Lord. I'd typically thought of an accountability partner as a particularly close friend, usually of the same gender, who might sometimes (in a loving way) get in my face and ask tough questions about how my personal life is going. An accountability partner might ask questions about my relationship to God, how I'm doing at loving my spouse and children, how I'm handling work, etc. This is a person who is, in a way, responsible for keeping me on track. And by the same token, I would be, at least in part, responsible to keep this friend on track.

One day at my breakfast table, "accountability partner" took on a whole new meaning for me. My children came trotting in, sat down, and looked at me—just looked

GOD IS NOT concerned about speed reading or how I measure up when compared to other believers.

at me. Suddenly, without warning, I felt incredibly accountable—and not just to one person but four.

Of course my kids aren't accountability partners who confront me with questions about my personal life. They're not really allowed to get in Mom's face. No, this accountability is more like responsibility. They look to me, and I am keenly aware that I am responsible (at least in part) to teach them the truth. Knowing this makes me want to be consistent in reading the Bible to them. It also cautions me not to elaborate on our reading beyond what I know. The sense of responsibility pushes me to seek help when we come across passages I don't understand.

And here's the big one: my children are watching me (and Wes). They want to see how I am responding to the truth we read in God's Word. They want to know if I will obey what I read. I must admit that I often fail, and my children are even watching to see how I handle the failure.

Now I realize this whole accountability thing may not sound fun. It may even sound ominously heavy, burdensome. But I've found that the accountability is actually a blessing. My accountability before my children has increased my motivation to be consistent in reading the Bible. And the more I get to know God through His Word, the more I see this accountability/responsibility intersecting with His grace. This discipline of studying God's Word that could so easily seem like a duty has become a delight. The Bible reading that used to be motivated by guilt is now motivated by joyful devotion.

MEALTIMES ARE GREAT TIMES

They were continually devoting themselves
to the apostles' teaching and to fellowship,
to the breaking of bread and to prayer.
Acts 2:42

Over the past few years, Wes and I have discovered that breakfast, lunch, and dinner are more than just times to eat. They're important times for us to spend together as a family. They're great opportunities for fellowship and for building family unity.

There's a bond that occurs when people gather around food. This is no less true in our immediate family. When we sit down to a meal, we laugh together, make plans together, share our thoughts, sometimes air our frustrations, and, yes, we eat. We have great memories of times shared around the table.

When I started reading the Bible with the kids, I chose to read at breakfast because it was a natural time for us to gather. In the beginning, part of my thinking was that the kids would have their mouths full and they would be quiet while I read. This is still part of my approach. But there was more to the choice of breakfast time than that. Sitting around the table, we connect. We connect over the food and the Bible.

I chose to memorize verses at lunch because it was another natural time for us to be together. As my children have gotten older and become involved in more activities, practicing memory verses over lunchtime has been more difficult to maintain. We have stopped and started memorizing many times. I have learned, however, that if I don't set a consistent time to work on memorizing Scripture, it won't ever happen. The great thing about attaching this practice to a meal is that it helps establish a regular routine. Going over the passage we're memorizing doesn't take very long, and it makes a great conversation-starter. And eating while memorizing makes the discipline that much more enjoyable.

While breakfast and lunch are great times, our evening meal is the day's pinnacle. Why? Because Dad is there! During our evening meal, the entire family reconnects at the end of a busy day. We talk, plan, report on the day, and laugh. And because we're together, even the quality of the food seems bumped up a notch. Dinnertime has become the most natural time for Wes to help our family understand how to live our lives in light of the good news of Jesus. It's not a forced or awkward gathering of the family, and so it's not intimidating. We can listen and ask questions, discuss and apply God's Word, all while we are bonding together over food.

Now before you get in your head that we have this ideal family where mealtime is always a feast characterized by grand discussions, let me point out that we are pretty normal. Sometimes we're eating leftover surprise and everyone has his or her own agenda for the conversation. Other times we're wolfing down bowls of cold cereal before we pile into the car to get to some event for which we are already late.

At times we miss our breakfast Bible reading or forget to go over our verse at lunch or rush out the door after an all-too-quick dinner. But meals together have become a great blessing as we've made them a priority. We have come to cherish those times when God has linked our hearts together and linked our hearts to His, as we gathered around a meal.

READING ALOUD HELPS ME

They read from the book, from the law of God, translating to give the sense so that they understood the reading. Nehemiah 8:8

I have always heard that reading to your children is extremely beneficial for them. For example, reading aloud to your children increases their vocabulary, improves their attention spans, and engages their minds and imaginations. And obviously the benefits are multiplied when you are reading to your children the most important words ever written.

Seldom, however, do I hear of the benefits experienced by the parents who are doing the reading, but they are just as numerous. Here are a few I have discovered.

First, when I am reading the Bible aloud, I stay awake. You may laugh, but how many times have you been quietly reading the Bible only to wake up? My mind stays engaged when I am reading out loud—even to my little audience. I admit there have been a handful of moments when I have said, "Hey guys, I need to read that sentence over. My mind drifted." But those moments are rare. I am alert, engaged, and focused when I am reading the Bible aloud.

I have also become a better reader by reading out loud. I don't just mean the ability to read, although I do think reading aloud every day for several years would improve anyone's reading. I am referring more to the ability to convey a story. I tend to be rather monotonic when I read quietly in my head. When I read the Bible to my children, I reach to find the tone and inflections in a passage, which helps me deliver the story.

Getting a better feel for the tone of a given passage has also helped us understand the setting for the

I GET TO SEE when they are surprised or the "aha" moment when the lightbulb has finally come on.

story and what is being conveyed. When I read Luke 10, where the disciples returned to Jesus rejoicing and saying, "Even the demons are subject to us in Your name," and Christ responded by saying, "I was watching Satan fall from heaven like lightning," I knew there is no way that Christ said that in a monotonic voice! I don't think I fully appreciated the enthusiasm, delight, and encouragement in His words until I read this passage aloud. My children appreciated it, too. My son looked completely amazed and said, "I didn't know Jesus encouraged people."

I notice more details when I read out loud. When I read silently I can read right past some interesting wording and details, like the fact that Ezekiel repeatedly uses the phrase "the word of the Lord came to me saying." And I'm not the only one noticing. As we were reading Ezekiel, it got to the point where I could just sit down and before I opened my mouth, my kids would automatically say, "The word of the Lord came to me saying." We heard those words day after day!

I've heard that people retain information better when

they engage more than one sense. When I look with my eyes at the written Word of God and also hear His words with my ears, these words are reinforced in me. I, for one, need that double whammy.

I'll mention one more benefit to reading the Bible aloud to my children. I get a lot of pleasure from watching my audience. I get to see their faces when they are surprised by some event in the Bible, or the puzzled looks when they don't understand, or the "aha" moment when I can tell the lightbulb has finally come on. I get to witness the Holy Spirit opening their minds and hearts.

Reading the Bible out loud is extremely beneficial— not just for the one who receives the Word but for the one who is delivering the Word as well.

I LEARN TO LISTEN

"Truly I say to you, whoever does not receive the kingdom of God like a child will not enter it at all."
Luke 18:17

If you think it's amazing that my very young children stopped talking long enough to listen to me read chapters from God's Word, you're right. What's even more amazing is that sometimes I stopped talking, or reading, long enough to listen to them talk! A lot of times our morning went something like this.

"Hey guys, come sit down. It's time for breakfast."

We sit around the table, stomachs growling. I lead us

in prayer, and then as soon as I say "Amen," they dive into the food and one of my kids has a story to tell. "Last night at small group Brendon got the plunger and was riding it like a stick horse. It was hilarious."

Then another story: "Luke is so easy to scare. All you have to do is walk up behind him and go 'boo' and he jumps."

I tell my kids they really shouldn't go around scaring Luke, then I wait for the next story. And inevitably it comes. Eventually, the storytelling must come to an end. I rein in the conversation and start reading our chapter of the Bible.

This process used to frustrate me a bit. It seemed to take such a long time for us to get to our one chapter. But I have come to realize that sometimes my children need to talk. Apparently, they've built up all these words during the night and they have to let some out. When they release a little (not all but a little), I can see by the expressions on their faces that they are glad I listened. And I know that, having expressed themselves a bit, they will be a bit less distracted as they listen to me.

This does not mean that they never interrupt while I am reading. They do—quite often. At first I was quick to hush them, but I soon learned that their input is often helpful. Sometimes it's only by the interruption that I can tell whether they are or are not understanding what I'm reading. Many times one of my children will have a great question to ask or an insight to share.

Emma, our youngest, often wants to know what some word in our reading means. She's simply trying to get a better idea of what's happening in the narrative. Not long ago she asked me what the word *incense* means. When I explained, I realized she was not the only one who didn't know. It benefited us all to stop and discuss the meaning of that word. One morning, all my kids wanted me to explain *atonement*. I stopped to look it up in a dictionary that I keep handy. In the end, I, too, had a better definition of *atonement*.

Other times one of the children interrupts because he finds some detail interesting or she has something insightful to add. These "interruptions" have a way of connecting what we're reading to reality, *our* reality.

One morning I was reading Luke 16, where Jesus tells the story of the rich man and Lazarus. The rich man lived in luxury and splendor while Lazarus, the poor man, was sick and hungry at the rich man's gate. I'll pick up the text in verse 22:

> Now the poor man died and was carried away by the angels to Abraham's bosom; and the rich man also died and was buried. In Hades he lifted up his eyes, being in torment, and saw Abraham far away and Lazarus in his bosom. And he cried out and said, "Father Abraham, have mercy on me."

At that point, Benjamin, who appeared to be engrossed in a battle with a handful of army men, perked up and said, "Isn't it interesting that the rich man calls Abraham 'Father,' I mean, considering where he is."

I started to continue reading, but I had to pause and admit, "That *is* interesting." I would have read right over that detail without giving it much thought if Benjamin had not pointed it out. We took a moment to discuss why the rich man would have called Abraham "Father."

Of course there are also times when I am reading and one child just stops to ask if I can get the butter, or a child might ask to be excused right in the middle of our reading. There are moments when they just get giggly with one another, and I have to say, "Guys, focus!" But even those are worthwhile moments, because they're learning what I'm learning: that they *can* focus their attention.

But I've learned to open my ears to what these young ones have to say because there are *many* moments when their helpful and insightful questions and comments prompt great discussion that sharpens us all. I don't want to squelch those moments.

READING WITH MY CHILDREN IS FUN

A joyful heart is good medicine. Proverbs 17:22

One afternoon while I was taking a shower . . . er, let me pause here for a moment. If you're a mom of little ones, you may understand that as much as you would like to get a shower first thing every morning, sometimes it just doesn't happen. So you get a shower when you can. At my house I have certain rules while Mom is in the shower, and all the kids know the rules.

When the kids were younger, one rule I followed was always to leave the bathroom door unlocked in case of an emergency. They knew to knock and then come in and let me know if there was some kind of disaster. (Nowadays the bathroom door is locked, so they just knock and yell details of the crisis through the door.) In all my years as a parent, there has yet to be a bona fide emergency, but when the kids were small I rarely took a shower without some child *thinking* there was an emergency. I have settled many disputes from behind that curtain. It was actually remarkable for me to shower without some sort of "intermission." One particular afternoon, however, it was well worth the disturbance.

For a brief time my shower featured just me and my Dial soap, when all of a sudden the door swung open and

WHEN I AM reading the Bible aloud, I stay awake.

I heard my five-year-old son, Graham, yell, "Mom!!" Then total silence. After this mysterious pause, he announced, with some confusion in his voice, "There's a cloud in here." From behind my curtain, I was attempting to describe how hot water produces steam when he exclaimed, "I thought God had descended on the temple!" We had been reading about Solomon dedicating the temple and how the cloud had filled the temple. It was in his mind, and it just popped out of his mouth, much to the astonishment of his mother.

While I was encouraged that our Bible reading had lingered in my son's mind, that's not the main reason I tell that story. I tell it because it's funny. It did not take long for me to discover that reading the Bible with my children is fun.

Our family can't count the number of times our Bible reading has produced giggles or full-fledged laugh riots. It happens all the time! Sometimes we laugh as we misunderstand a word or phrase or sentence and then figure it out. Sometimes we laugh because there's such a culture jump between contemporary America and the Bible-times culture of a story we're reading.

Sometimes Wes and I just crack up over the way our children's little minds process what we read. Once, after we'd been reading Romans 3, Benjamin announced, "Romans is short . . . *and deep.*" I laughed out loud, in part over hearing such a statement come out of a little guy, but also because, in a weird sort of way, the statement was profound.

The laughter is certainly not because we don't love and honor God's Word and take it seriously. We do respect and prize the Scriptures; that's what the whole venture is about! It's more that we are finding ourselves at home with reading God's Word and enjoying one another's company.

My children made me laugh the day we reached Mark 12. In verse 13, religious leaders begin taking turns asking Jesus questions in an attempt to trap Him in His statements. By verse 18 the Sadducees take their turn at trying to trick Jesus.

The Sadducees come to Jesus, saying,

"Teacher, Moses wrote for us that if a man's brother dies and leaves behind a wife and leaves no child, his brother should marry the wife and raise up children to his brother."

Then they posed a situation to Jesus. Note that part of the trap here is that the Sadducees didn't believe in a future resurrection.

"There were seven brothers; and the first took a wife, and died leaving no children. The second one married her, and died leaving behind no children; and the third likewise; and so all seven left no children. Last of all, the woman died also. In the resurrection, when they rise again, which one's wife will she be? For all seven married her."

My children were following along with the reasoning in this tricky question and were curious to know what Jesus' answer would be. So I read:

"Is this not the reason you are mistaken, that you do not understand the Scriptures or the power of God? For when they rise from the dead they will neither marry, nor are given in marriage."

I had to stop there for a moment to take in the spectacle at my table. Maggie was on one side of the table, and Graham was seated directly opposite her. As I read the words "when they rise from the dead, they neither marry nor are given in marriage," Maggie's little face dropped in disappointment and she gave a loud "Aw!" while simultaneously Graham bounced in his chair, thrust his fist in the air, and shouted "Yes!" There they sat, Maggie frowning in disappointment and Graham grinning from ear to ear.

It was a funny moment as I watched my young daughter and young son (extremely young at this point) react very differently. I realized it is a tricky passage and we need to get the point of it straight, but sometimes it's good just to enjoy those memorable kid moments. We need those fun times of reading God's Word together.

When I began this journey, I thought God had given me this desire to read His Word at such an ironic time. My children were so young, and I was busier than I had ever been before. My days were filled with diaper changing, clothes washing, and preparing what seemed like one endless meal. I played tea party and built with blocks and looked at books that had only pictures. I could not have chosen a more peculiar time to become a consistent student of the Bible.

Now I stand in awe of God's timing. God used these four fun, curious, playful little people to help me experience the immense joy of getting to know God through His Word. I know that the Bible is not to be taken lightly. I know that what Jesus did for me is serious business. But I also know that "a joyful heart is good medi-cine" (Proverbs 17:22). Oh, what good medicine it has been for me!

Psalm 127:3 says, "Behold, children are a gift of the Lord." *Thank You, Lord, for my four amazing little gifts!*

THEY REALLY GET IT!

From childhood you have known the sacred writings which are able to give you the wisdom that leads to salvation through faith which is in Christ Jesus. 2 Timothy 3:15

One surprising aspect of reading the Bible to my children is the level of understanding they demonstrate. They don't understand everything all the time. I don't understand everything all the time myself! However, I have seen in the children, at various times, a growing capacity to understand God's Word.

God (obviously) knows that children have the capacity to learn and understand, and as I have read the Bible I have seen evidence that God intends for us as parents to teach our children His Word. Deuteronomy 6:7 says, with regard to the Israelites teaching God's commands to their children, "You shall teach them diligently to your sons and shall talk of them when you sit in your house and

 **NEW GENERATIONS** of children would "hear and learn to fear the Lord."

when you walk by the way and when you lie down and when you rise up." In other words, teach them the law as you are with them all throughout the day.

Nehemiah 8 tells how the priest Ezra read God's law to the people of Israel who had returned from exile.

> Then Ezra the priest brought the law before the assembly of men, women and *all who could listen with understanding*, on the first day of the seventh month. (emphasis mine)

Ezra read the law to the people, and the other priests who were with him went around explaining what had been read (a role I often play in our morning reading). The next day Ezra and the leaders of Israel gathered to examine the law further and were prompted to reinstitute the Feast of Booths, something the Israelites had long neglected to observe.

If you follow the cross-reference in your Bible for Nehemiah 8:2, it will take you to Deuteronomy 31, where Moses gave the original commands regarding this festival:

> When all Israel comes to appear before the Lord your God at the place which He will choose, you shall read this law in front of all Israel in their hearing. Assemble the people, the men and the women and *children* and the alien who is in your town, in order that they may hear and learn and fear the Lord your God, and be careful to observe all the words of this law. Their *children*, who have not known, will hear and learn to fear the Lord your God. (Deuteronomy 31:11–13, emphasis mine)

At this public reading of God's Word, new generations of children would "hear and learn to fear the Lord."

One morning the children and I were reading in Exodus 21. This passage follows the Ten Commandments and describes various laws given to the people of Israel. This is admittedly difficult reading. So I was reading the various laws and attempting to explain as best I could, when we came to verse 15, which says, "He who strikes his father or his mother shall surely be put to death." Wow! Then verse 17 says, "He who curses his father or his mother shall surely be put to death." I pointed out that some translations note that the word *curses* could be translated *dishonors*. Double wow!

I pointed out that God must take honoring your father and mother pretty seriously, and I mentioned that I could remember times when I had not honored my parents as I should. That was when my older son asked, "Is giving Grandma a coffee mug that says 'Grumpy' on it dishonoring?"

Ouch!

I don't want you to think I'm out to raise children bound by legalism, unable to have fun and enjoy a sense of humor. We gave the coffee mug to Grandma in a lighthearted way, and I believe that is the way she received it.

Yet I do want to raise children who read the Word of God and evaluate their actions and their motives as God gives them understanding. I want them to say to the Lord, "Search me, O God, and know my heart; try me and know my anxious thoughts; and see if there be any hurtful way in me, and lead me in the everlasting way" (Psalm 139:23–24).

That morning Graham had some insight about how much God wants us to honor our father and mother (and grandfather and grandmother). He was attempting to get at the heart of what it means to honor, and he wanted to make sure our family's conscience was clear before God.

Wes and I want to do our best (deficient as that may sometimes be) to put God's Word before our children and guide and teach them as we get up in the morning, as we sit down at breakfast, as we ride in the car, as we walk through the neighborhood, as we sit down at dinner, and as we lie down to rest at night. And we trust the Holy Spirit to shed light on the Word and give understanding, that we and our children may hear and learn and fear the Lord.

PARENTAL GUIDANCE IS SUGGESTED

Discretion will guard you, understanding
will watch over you. Proverbs 2:11

"Don't repeat this word anywhere. The only time you should say this word is right here, or if you have a question you can ask Dad or me. But never repeat this word to anyone else." I can't possibly count the number of times statements like these have come out of my mouth since we started reading the Bible.

I rapidly discovered that the Old Testament can be incredibly graphic. There are both mature themes in these Scriptures and words with which my children were, I'm glad to say, not familiar. After about half a dozen scenarios where I came upon a decidedly detailed passage and panicked, as I tried to think fast and explain it on a preschooler's level, I realized I needed a strategy.

For one thing, I needed to come up with some careful word definitions. I could simply explain some words— *circumcision, bosom, vomit,* and the like. After a giggle or an "Ooh, gross!" we could just go on with our reading. There were a couple of words I opted to omit altogether.

For other words, I wanted a definition that helped my kids understand the point of a story yet limited their exposure to sin or concepts they weren't yet ready to take in. My kids were just not mature enough to handle a complete explanation. I came up with definitions suitable for their age. A *virgin*, I explained, is a woman who has never been married. A *prostitute* is a woman who goes from one man to another and to another, instead of marrying one man and staying faithful to him. A *whore* (this word is used frequently in the Prophets) is similar to a prostitute and is most often used to describe how the children of Israel chased after other gods, instead of remaining faithful to the one true God.

Not only are there explicit words in Scripture, but there are also stories with very mature themes. Let's face it: the Bible is true and it's about real people. So it includes the beauty of intimacy as well as the reality of sin.

However, my little audience was small, innocent children. By *innocent*, I don't mean that they are not sinners; they are. They were born sinners. But they are naïve, and, frankly, I'd like to keep them that way. I want them "to be wise in what is good and innocent in what is evil" (Romans 16:19). Yet the Bible reveals to us, sometimes in candid terms, both good and evil.

So my strategy had to include how to handle violence, sex, and topics like the use of alcohol. We parents all have to deal with these topics anyway, and I would certainly rather deal with them within the context of Scripture, but I felt I needed a plan.

So I started scanning ahead. After we finished each day's reading, I would take a brief moment to glance over the next chapter to see what was coming. This was primarily to give me a little advance notice before I reached something explicit, so I could plan my approach.

My desire was not to add to or take away from Scripture but only to adjust a few stories to fit the maturity level of my children. Most often this was as simple as explaining a word on their level, omitting a word, or summarizing a sentence or a brief passage in my own words. I didn't want to load my young children with words and information that they might not know how to use wisely.

Wes and I have grown in our knowledge of how to approach these topics with our children and in discerning when each child is mature enough to handle more information. As the maturity level and flow of information increases, so the depth of understanding of the Bible and our Lord grows as well. This is a wonderful process to watch unfold.

LET THEM BE KIDS

Just as a father has compassion on his
children, so the Lord has compassion on
those who fear Him. Psalm 103:13

After reading about several kings of Israel who did what was evil and provoked the Lord to anger, we came to 1 Kings 16. Here Ahab becomes king, and we are quickly informed that he did more to provoke the anger of the Lord than all the kings of Israel who were before him. Scary!

As I came to the end of the chapter, I noticed Benjamin had finished his breakfast and was holding on to the edge of the table while balancing on a soccer ball. He was doing an extraordinary job of keeping himself upright on this ball, and I was doing an unusually good job of ignoring him. When I finished reading, he started humming, "If I Were a Rich Man" from *Fiddler on the Roof*. (This was completely unrelated to our reading.) I couldn't help but laugh out loud; it was funny.

There have been plenty of mornings when I have lost my patience because the kids would not sit still. I have to

remind myself of those first three days of reading Genesis when I didn't think they were listening and recognize
again that I am reading to small children. Not only that,
but I am reading some pretty heavy stuff to small children.
And on top of all that, I know I have a tendency to push
hard against the limits of their attention spans. Ac-
knowledging these facts helps me relax. I can grant my children a little freedom, freedom to be kids.

Some of my children actually listen better when they
have their hands (or feet) occupied with something else.
I require Benjamin, for example, to stay in the room, but
often it's hard for him to sit straight in a chair and do nothing. And even though Benjamin was balancing on a soccer
ball, I really believe he *was* listening—because it wasn't
until *after I finished reading* that he started humming.

MISSING A DAY DOES NOT MEAN FAILURE

I will give them a heart to know Me,
for I am the Lord. Jeremiah 24:7

One of the best things I did before we started reading
was make a plan. I had never before made a *specific* plan
when I had attempted to read the Bible. My plan was simple (and it fit our family): one chapter of the Bible a day,
five days a week, with the goal of reading the entire Bible,
from Genesis to Revelation, together with our children.

My plan had another vital feature: sick days. Back
when I had tried to calculate how long it would take us to

read through the Bible, I factored in sick days—days when we might not be able to read.

I can honestly say that since we began reading the Bible together, there has not been a day when I did not *want* to read to my children. That remarkable statement amazes even me, considering that I had never before successfully maintained a consistent time in God's Word and I had often not wanted to read my Bible. So the idea that God could fuel in me a desire to read His Word and maintain that desire over the long haul is nothing short of miraculous.

But there have been days when we could not read—but not usually because we were sick. When we were sick, most often we continued our reading and it was good for us. I remember one morning when we were all feeling sick. Benjamin and Emma had come down with the flu the day before, and by the next morning the rest of us were moaning and groaning as we pulled ourselves out of bed. Although not feeling his best, Wes went off to work while the kids and I sat down to breakfast. After we took turns complaining about our achy bodies, it was time to read. On that morning, we were reading Psalm 41:

How blessed is he who considers the helpless;
the Lord will deliver him in a day of trouble.
The Lord will protect him and keep him alive,
and he shall be called blessed upon the earth;
and do not give him over to the desires of his
enemies.
The Lord will sustain him upon his sickbed;
in his illness, You restore him to health.

We were all in somewhat of a daze, so I asked the kids, "Did you hear that?" Then I read that last verse again: *The Lord will sustain him upon his sickbed; In his illness, You restore him to health."*

My older son perked up and said, "Hey, we're sick today."

I responded, "Isn't it amazing that we read this particular verse today?" We stopped and thanked God for reminding us that He can sustain us and restore us to health. And we asked God to help us be the kind of person described in verse 1.

So, you might ask, when did we use our sick days? We used them when our daily routine changed. For example, when we were on vacation, had company, or went to visit family, the "sick days" became important.

Factoring in those "off" days gave me a big-picture perspective on Bible reading. Seeking God through His Word is a lifetime endeavor. As with any lifetime endeavor, there will likely come days when we can't do what we normally do. For once, I had essentially planned ahead for that day. So when we missed a day or two, or even a week or two, of our routine, it did not mean we had failed. It was not the end of our Bible reading. When life got back to normal, we picked up where we left off in our reading.

The sick days have reminded me that flawlessly carrying out the plan is not the goal. Of course I need to consistently read and study the Bible to mature in my faith, but I also recognize that my assimilation of God's Word is a work of God. Reading the entire Bible is a goal, but it is not *the* goal. The goal is knowing God.

BE REAL WITH MY CHILDREN

Therefore let us draw near with confidence to the throne of grace, so that we may receive mercy and find grace to help in time of need. Hebrews 4:16

After several years of reading, we reached Mark 2, the story of Jesus healing the paralytic. By the time I'd read four verses, I was so choked up I could hardly read. There are moments when God's Word pierces right to the heart. It was one of those mornings.

Four men carried a paralyzed friend to where Jesus was teaching. When they reached the overcrowded house and couldn't get through the door, they didn't say, "Oh, Jesus probably wouldn't have healed him anyway. Let's go

AS GOD RENOVATES my heart, I can't know or guess when He will stir my children's hearts as well.

home." No! They climbed up on the roof, carrying their suffering friend on his mat and dug a hole in the top of someone else's house, desperate to reach the One they were convinced could heal their friend. They really believed—and they really loved their friend.

This kind of faith made me take a look at my own faith, and I began to cry. When Jesus saw the faith of the four, He did more than they expected. He didn't just heal their friend's legs, He forgave his sins.

My throat felt tight. I was straining through tear-filled eyes to see the words on the page. My young children were watching with serious expressions, when all of a sudden Maggie blurted, "You look sick or something."

I tried to explain my condition. Though they looked at me with a great deal of sympathy, we were not really "on the same page." They were not experiencing the conviction I was experiencing. I was seeing how weak my faith is compared to these four friends, as well as my lack of boldness in approaching Jesus, who is able to heal and forgive.

My kids didn't fully understand my response. Some mornings are like that. God doesn't always work on all of us in the same way or at the same time. I may experience great conviction, while my children are spectators. However, I've learned not to hide those moments from them. My children need to see what repentance is like. There are times when I need to be transparent, so that they can see God's Word at work in me. As God renovates my heart, I can't know or guess when He will stir their hearts as well.

PRAY

We all, with unveiled face, beholding as in a mirror the glory of the Lord, are being transformed into the same image from glory to glory, just as from the Lord, the Spirit. 2 Corinthians 3:18

When we started Genesis, I felt overwhelmed. The idea of reading the entire Bible was intimidating—and the task seemed compounded by the fact that my children were between about nine months and four years of age. But through prayer God had fueled my desire for His Word. As we began reading, I continually realized how much more I needed to call out to Him.

I prayed these two requests almost every morning of the *whole* five years of our first reading of the Bible: "Lord, allow my children and me to remember more than we think we are capable of remembering. And Lord, let us understand more than we think we are capable of understanding."

When we were close to the finish line, however, I heard a sermon that modified my prayers. Our pastor preached on how the Word of God penetrates a life. He illustrated the point by drawing concentric circles. The outer circle illustrated how the Word first enters our lives, and the inner circle showed the deepest level of entry, the target. The outer circle was labeled "Perceive" (or hear) and the next circle in was labeled "Understand." I recognized that I had been praying, almost exactly, those two outer circles.

But in my pastor's illustration, those two outer circles weren't the bull's-eye. When God's Word penetrates deeper, a person responds in belief, obeying what he's heard and understood. That obedience leads to transformation—into the image of Christ.

As I heard this message, I realized that transforming was exactly what I wanted God's Word to do in my life, in my husband's life, and in the lives of our children.

I still pray that God will help us all to

hear and remember and understand the Word of God. But now each morning I include something like this: "Dear God, be near to us today as we read Your Word. Holy Spirit, open the Word to us and teach us. Give us the ability to remember and understand more than we think we are capable of. Help us to believe what we read today and give us the desire and strength to obey Your commands. Use Your Word to transform us into the image of Christ. Please hear our prayer, and move and work in our lives today. We ask this in Jesus' name. Amen."

So let it be!

What Next?
What Happens When We Cross the Finish Line

9

I have no greater joy than this, to hear of my children walking in the truth.
3 John 4

I was forty-one when I completed my first reading of the entire Bible. I have mixed feelings about that. I can't help wishing I'd formed the habit earlier in my life. However, most of the time, my disappointment quickly gets eclipsed by the immense gratitude I feel for the grace God has shown to me.

During a crazy busy season of life, when consistent Bible reading should have seemed impossible, God gave me a hunger to know Him and a simple plan of reading His Word with my kids. And to my surprise, more than anyone's, we did it. Together, we read the entire Bible.

As we were reading Revelation, I began to ask, "What next?"

GOD WILL BE right there with you, doing something much bigger than you.

I tossed around several decent ideas. I considered the possibility that we might need a little break from reading. I thought about reading a Christian biography at breakfast. I even thought about attempting a history lesson on the early church.

Then Wes chimed in, "You should just start over—the next day!"

I immediately recognized that this was a better idea.

We didn't want our children to get the notion that you read the Bible once and then check it off your list. We wanted their appetites for God to grow. We wanted them to hear God speak. We wanted them to develop a thriving relationship with Jesus. So it made sense for us to keep reading the Bible.

When the time came, I was so happy to have finally read the entire Bible that I honestly couldn't wait to start again. So the day after we finished Revelation, we started over with Genesis 1. We did decide to read a different translation. The first trip through, we read the New American Standard Bible. This time we chose the English Standard Version. My oldest three kids were excited for their younger sister, Emma, who would be hearing parts of the Bible she had never heard before because she wasn't yet born when we began the first reading.

Our attention spans had grown (including mine!), and on most days we were able to handle more than one chapter. The Holy Spirit continued to open our minds and increase our understanding. My kids would often perk up when we came to a passage they remembered from our first reading. And yes, they still acted out stories from time to time. Sometimes they even recruited me to take a part.

With older listeners and a more experienced mom, the second adventure through all of Scripture seemed to move quickly. In three years we completed our second reading.

We are currently on our third journey through God's Word.

My kids are not toddlers anymore—my oldest has hit the teen years—so the acting has been replaced with perceptive questions that prompt great discussion. I still have a lot of opportunities to say, "Maybe Dad can help us with this one."

We're pausing over words and phrases we simply didn't notice during the first two readings. My children are connecting different parts of Scripture and getting excited when they learn something new. I never cease to be amazed at how God continues to speak to us through His Word.

Most of the stories I have shared come from the days of our first reading of the Bible. Each story has become a marker, a memory to ponder in my heart. I remember the first time we read Nehemiah. I took in a vivid and much-needed picture of God's mercy for sinners like me.

Ezra, the scribe and priest, reads the book of the law to the exiles who had returned to Jerusalem. He stands up on a platform with some other men, and they read the law from early in the morning until midday. The people stand—apparently enthralled—during the entire reading. Next Ezra, Nehemiah, and some of the Levites help the people make sense of what they had heard.

> Then Nehemiah, who was the governor, and Ezra the priest and scribe, and the Levites who taught the people said to all the people, "This day is holy to the Lord your God; do not mourn or weep." *For all the people were weeping when they heard the words of the law.* (Nehemiah 8:9, emphasis mine)

When these exiles heard and began to understand God's law, *they wept.* God's Word penetrated their hearts.

I can only imagine they were experiencing a deep sense of conviction.

As I read, I started to tear up. My kids had those uneasy expressions that kids get when they think Mom is about to cry. They were looking at me as if to say, "Why are you crying? They just said *not* to cry."

When the people heard God's Word, they understood what He required and that they didn't measure up—and they cried. I could relate. I was endeavoring to read the entire Bible for the first time. I was encountering portions of God's Word I had never read before. There were aspects of God's character being revealed that I had never known. There were pictures of Christ I had never seen. Like the people gathered before Ezra and Nehemiah, I wanted to cry.

The Israelites' mourning was a right response before God, and so was mine. I needed to confess how I had sinned by not seeking to know God through His Word.

But like the exiles, I heard these words: *"Do not mourn or weep."* Isn't God's mercy amazing? He didn't push His people down; He lifted them up.

Not only were God's wayward people not to mourn or weep, but they were to celebrate as God intended. This was a time for joy in the Lord.

Then he said to them, "Go, eat of the fat, drink of the sweet, and send portions to him who has nothing prepared; for this day is holy to our Lord. Do not be grieved, for the joy of the Lord is your strength." So the Levites calmed all the people, saying, "Be still, for the day is holy; do not be grieved." *All the people went away to eat, to drink, to send portions and to celebrate a great festival, because they understood the words which had been made known to them.* (Nehemiah 8:10–12, emphasis mine)

The people celebrated—not just because they had plenty to eat and drink and share but because they understood God's Word.

During my first reading of the Bible, there were times when I read a part of God's Word I had never read before and I felt ashamed. This was a right response. There is a time for mourning. I needed to acknowledge my sin and change some practices in my life.

I also needed to celebrate God's mercy. I had to strengthen myself in the joy of the Lord. Matthew Henry says in his commentary, "To have the Holy Scriptures with us, and help to understand them, is a very great mercy, which we have abundant reason to rejoice in."

God has given me a new hunger to know Him through

His Word. And He is helping me to understand. This is truly a time to rejoice.

And my rejoicing has been multiplied. God has taken my past failure in studying the Bible, flipped it upside down, and is using it for the good of us all. That is so like God! Only He can take the years I thought were lost and redeem them. Every morning around our table, I experience God's redeeming grace. I get to be an instrument to deliver good news to my kids and show them the way to real joy. And every time I see one of my children's faces light up because they understand, I go away rejoicing.

IT'S NOT TOO LATE . . .
AND IT'S NOT TOO EARLY

Be encouraged. God wants to reveal Himself to you through His Word. He can and will speak to your children.

If you already have a thriving consistent time in God's Word, I commend you. Keep seeking God. Or maybe, like me, you've struggled to keep on reading. You feel guilty and frustrated. I understand. But I am confident that if God can sustain in me a desire to read His Word, He can do this for you as well.

God used an extended season of prayer in my life to reveal my need for Him and to grow in me a hunger to know Him through His Word. He created in me a desire, not to fulfill a requirement but to get to know the God of the universe.

You can't go wrong with prayer. So before you pick up your Bible to try again, spend some time talking to God. Ask Him to give you a desire, a hunger, to know Him. Trust that "He who began a good work in you will perfect it until the day of Christ Jesus" (Philippians 1:6).

When you do pick up your Bible, throw away any ideas about speed-reading or measuring up to other Christian friends. This is about taking in the living and active Word of our Lord. Take your time. Focus on Him.

And while you're considering how to get God's Word in you, turn your attention to that little guy running around your living room wielding a sippy cup or that playful girl out swinging in your backyard. Look at the little people building Lego towers on your kitchen table. Dream about what God wants to do in your children— and how He longs to use you to draw them to Himself. You can be a tool that God molds and shapes and uses to affect the next generation right there at your feet.

If you don't already have a plan to get God's Word in your kids, make one. Remember Augustine's words: "When we read Scripture, God speaks to us." You can be the one giving them the very words of God.

I'm just beginning to comprehend the amazing opportunity we have, as moms, to impact the lives of our kids. We have a window of opportunity to saturate them in love and truth. We won't do it perfectly, and we will have to ask for forgiveness over and over. But we also won't be alone. God is with us, and He loves us. Jesus gave Himself for you and me and is, even now, interceding for us. The Spirit is empowering us from within. And God's Word will prevail.

My passion for reading the Bible with my kids has grown in recent years, in many ways because of what Scripture itself says about what God's Word can do in their lives and mine. Just read this sampling of Scripture:

The law of the Lord is perfect, restoring the soul;
the testimony of the Lord is sure, making wise the
simple.
The precepts of the Lord are right, rejoicing the heart;
the commandment of the Lord is pure, enlightening
the eyes. (Psalm 19:7–8)

Your word I have treasured in my heart,
that I may not sin against You. (Psalm 119:11)

Your word is a lamp to my feet
and a light to my path. (Psalm 119:105)

Sanctify them in the truth; Your word is truth.
(John 17:17)

So faith comes from hearing, and hearing by the word of Christ. (Romans 10:17)

All Scripture is inspired by God and profitable for teaching, for reproof, for correction, for training in righteousness; so that the man of God may be adequate, equipped for every good work. (2 Timothy 3:16–17)

For the word of God is living and active and sharper than any two-edged sword, and piercing as far as the division of soul and spirit, of both joints and marrow, and able to judge the thoughts and intentions of the heart. (Hebrews 4:12)

I want God's Word to do its work in me, but I long even more for these promises of Scripture to be realized for my children. I want my kids to put their faith in Jesus and be strengthened in that faith. I want them to be prepared for every good work. I want my children to have a lamp and light to guide them along every path they will take. I want these things for my kids—and I *can't* accomplish them. But the Holy Spirit and the Word of God can.

YOU MAY BE feeling inadequate to teach God's Word to your children. I know how you feel.

What I *can* do is be their mom, fulfilling the calling God has given me. I can be an instrument, though frail and imperfect, God may use to bring my children to Him. I can love them, teach them, correct them, spend time with them, listen to them, pray for them, and read His Word with them. God can take that effort and do far more than I could imagine. *I am weak, but He is strong.*

I want to give you hope—hope that you can read the Bible together and that it is well worth the effort. If you're not currently reading the Bible with your children, won't you begin now? It will be messy and loud and sticky; it won't be picture-perfect. There will be days when you are impatient and your kids are restless. Some days it will be hard to keep going. But then there will be those other days, when God gives you a glimpse of what He is doing in the heart of your child.

God *will* speak to you through His Word. He will grow you and your children in wisdom and knowledge and the fear of the Lord. He will be right there with you, doing something much bigger than you.

I'm not usually a visionary person. I don't typically

 **MAY GOD BE** pleased to raise up a generation acquainted with Scripture since childhood, walking humbly with Him.

plan too far down the road. But it's worthwhile to envision ten, fifteen, or even twenty years down the road, when your kids have the Word of God in their minds and hearts and a mom who has been praying for them for years. Think about them leaving home, with lives built on the firm foundation of Jesus Christ. Imagine them knowing where to turn when they sin, having the assurance that Jesus is their only hope. Think about preparing them to go the distance by giving them "the sword of the Spirit, which is the word of God" (Ephesians 6:17). Consider how God could use your children, grounded in His Word, to glorify His name in the world.

You may be feeling inadequate to teach God's Word to your children. I know how you feel. But remember "Him who is able to do far more abundantly beyond all that we ask or think, according to the power that works within us" (Ephesians 3:20).

Grab those small hands that are growing so fast. Look in those cute little eyes that are soaking in so much of the world around them. Make the most of today. Read His Word together.

God took this slow reader—this undisciplined woman, this immature believer—and gave me a hunger to know Him. He's using me to teach my children, and my children to teach me. We're getting to know God through His Word.

Your circumstances and season of life will likely be different from mine, but God can put the desire in your heart and give you a plan that suits your family. Soon you will have your own stories, moments to treasure in your heart. And these markers will be fuel that God uses to keep you going.

May the Lord bless you and sustain you as you seek Him. May He be pleased to raise up a generation acquainted with Scripture since childhood, walking humbly with God.

The Together
Appendix

I often skip the appendix section in a book. Moms often don't have time to get lost in an appendix. With that in mind, I offer you this helpful, straight-to-the-point information designed to be a companion for you—to answer questions, encourage, and provide practical assistance.

So here are a few tips, resources, and questions to spark small group discussion. But remember, what you need most is just your Bible and your desire to seek the Lord. Simplicity is powerful—and a great tool for success.

Getting Started

Don't get bogged down with a heavy to-do list. The goal is to get reading! These are simple suggestions for preparing your heart and your family for daily Bible reading.

Pray. Ask God to give you and your children a hunger for the Word and desire to know Him.

Don't go it alone. If you are married, talk to your husband. Seek his input as you plan and ask him to join you in prayer. Ask your husband or a close friend, or both, to pray for your quest to grow your appetite for God. Ask for help in answering biblical and practical questions, too.

Evaluate. Assess your routine. Choose a time and place that suits the rhythm of your family. Aim for five days a week.

Consider. You might spend some time dipping into *How to Read the Bible for All Its Worth* (Zondervan), which provides a good, basic overview. But don't let reading this book delay you. Go ahead and start reading the Bible with your family. You can read this work along the way!

Be patient. It may take some time to find your "groove." Your reading time doesn't have to be picture-perfect. Just keep reading. Your attention spans and your appetite for God's Word will grow.

Keep Jesus central in all of your reading. All of Scripture was written to point to Jesus. Don't think that the Old Testament is just full of good stories and only some parts of it point to Jesus. *It's all about Him.* Develop a keen eye, and expect the Holy Spirit to show you how all your Bible is centralized around Jesus Christ.

Be okay with the "sweep" of Scripture. It may be in your nature to want to stop and study, answering all your theological questions as you read with your kids. I understand this, as I am also passionate to have and pass along sound doctrine and theology. But don't bog down your reading. Jot down your questions, and tackle them personally as you make time for that. Meanwhile, try to enjoy the big sweep, while you dig deeper at other times.

Pay no attention to the day's feelings. Pick up your Bible and read the next chapter (or however much you plan to read) even when you feel numb, distracted, angry, upset, sad, or anything else. When it seems that God is distant—and for that matter, your husband and children are, too—just keep reading.

Have fun. Enjoy the interaction with your children. Make this a special time that you and your children will look forward to.

Expect God to speak! I've said it before, but it's worth saying again. As you read, you're speaking aloud the very words of God in your home. *God is speaking every day that you read!* Grow in your wonder over having Him communicate to you. Come to your reading, *anticipating* and *expecting* that God will speak to you!

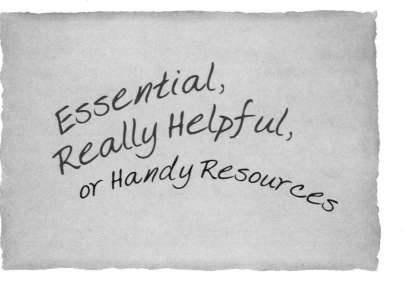

Essential, Really Helpful, or Handy Resources

*B*e careful! There are vast numbers of excellent books, blogs, articles, podcasts, and more to inspire and enlighten your reading of God's Word. But don't get lost in the sea of good things and miss the best thing—you, your kids, and the Bible.

Go ahead and check this stuff out, but don't get distracted from the simple purpose of getting to know God through His Word.

ESSENTIAL

The Bible. A good, faithful translation is really the main tool for this adventure. We'll talk about faithful Bible translations on page 173.

REALLY HELPFUL

A good dictionary. It's amazing how often I've had to look up words like *cubit* and *concubine.* If I take the time to look up a word (even when I think I know the definition), it gives my children a clearer explanation of the word and broadens my definition, as well.

A journal. Nothing fancy, just a place to write down thoughts you don't want to lose. Do it in a spiral notebook or on your smartphone.

HANDY BOOKS

A study Bible. A study Bible offers good introductions to each book of the Bible, notes that appear on the same page as the text to which they refer, thorough cross-references to lead you to parallel or linked passages, and more. It's great for finding a quick answer when you have a question about a particular verse or passage. My favorites are the *ESV Study Bible* and the *MacArthur Study Bible.*

A Bible dictionary. You'll find there are lots of distinctly biblical words your regular dictionary can't flesh out. There are many good ones, even some available online.

A pictorial Bible dictionary. Kids especially appreciate visual help for understanding what Mom is reading.

Our family has enjoyed **Zondervan's Pictorial Bible Dictionary**.

A one-volume commentary. Of course you can find numerous commentaries on every individual book of the Bible. But to keep things simple and the information less overwhelming, a commentary in one volume on the whole of Scripture is a great tool. I've appreciated **The MacArthur Bible Commentary, The New Bible Commentary**, and **Matthew Henry's Commentary**.

David C. Cook Journey through the Bible. This well-illustrated resource unpacks Bible stories for families.

How to Read the Bible for All Its Worth, by Gordon D. Fee and Douglas Stuart, which provides a beneficial overview of the types of books in the Bible, their intent for the original audience, and implications for us today.

CHILDREN'S RESOURCES
(that aren't just for kids!)

The Jesus Storybook Bible: Every Story Whispers His Name by Sally Lloyd-Jones. This is a great supplement to your daily Bible reading. You will love this storybook that clearly demonstrates that Jesus is the point of all of Scripture. This beautifully written and illustrated book will grow your desire to get to know Him!

Buck Denver Asks . . . What's in the Bible? DVD series from VeggieTales creator Phil Vischer gives kids an overview of Scripture. You'll be learning and laughing, too.

WEBSITES, LINKS, & APPS

Be sure to come to **www.aneverydaymama.com** for current lists of my favorite ministries, websites, links, smartphone/tablet apps, and more.

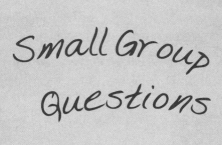

Small Group Questions

GROW APPETITES
FOR GOD TOGETHER

Whether you're just one-on-one with a friend or in a small group, here are some questions to get you going.

DISCUSSION 1

Introduction: Not-So-Quiet Times

1. What's one of the funniest things you've heard a kid say about the Bible?

2. What do you think about blending your personal Bible reading with reading aloud to your kids? How do

you feel about the whole "together" idea? Does it feel wrong, right, new?

3. Do you tend to look at your kids as obstacles who get in the way of your ability to read and study the Bible?

4. Tell about your successes and failures at Bible reading. Do you think a lot of women and moms feel like failures when it comes to the area of Bible reading and the "spiritual disciplines"? Do you feel guilty or like a failure?

5. Are you currently reading the Bible? What are the barriers to your consistency in reading? Why should consistency even be a goal?

6. What do you think about the statement, "My acceptance is not based on whether or not I have read the entire Bible"?

7. Honesty check: Do you find the Bible boring?

8. Think and talk about the heart and ways of God. Why is it not too late for you to start seeking Him through Scripture, and why is it never too early for your children to start?

DISCUSSION 2

Chapter 1
We Read the Bible:
And It Comes to Life

1. Have your ever read the Bible to your kids or to other kids? What was it like?

2. Would reading with your kids at breakfast work for your personal family rhythm? What would you need to shuffle? What are other times that might work for your family?

3. Carrie's first days of reading the Bible with her kids didn't go exactly as planned. Do you know what it's like to have big dreams that get met with reality? When has it happened to you?

4. This chapter describes shifting your expectation away from obsessing "over trying to get them to hang on every word." Can you lower this expectation? Does this bring some hope to you?

5. How do you see your role in helping your children understand the Bible?

6. Stop and pray that God would give you the desire to read His Word and that you would understand more

than you think you are capable of understanding.

7. How can kids' play reinforce what they're learning? What can we do as moms to help encourage the acting out—the visualizing—of Bible stories in our homes? How does seeing these scenes come alive in your home *strengthen and build* your faith?

8. How would you characterize your own mothering style—way laid-back to really rigid, or somewhere in between? Where do you need grace, in "lightening up" or in "getting more disciplined"? What's one biblical and practical thing you can do this week in order to grow?

DISCUSSION 3
Chapter 2
Moving Days: How God
Jump-Started Our Bible Reading

1. Icebreaker: How many times have you moved? What has been the good, bad, and ugly of moving?

2. What things have happened to you that simply floored you—took your breath away, felt like a body blow? What did that do to your thinking about God? About your life? About your family?

3. Have you experienced an extended time of crying out to God for help—and then had Him answer in a way you didn't expect—or want? When has God showed you more about Himself—and more about you?

4. How is it a *gracious* thing for God to reveal that your sin is "hideous and grievous to a holy and good God"?

5. Read aloud this excerpt from chapter 2:

After weeks of hearing what the Bible had to say about the fear of God, I was given a renewed sense of awe. I can remember standing in church holding back tears as we sang songs about the glory of God. I was flooded with the reality that this great God deserves reverence and worship. Jesus, my Savior, deserves my devotion.

How can a renewed fear of God like this kindle affection for His Word in you? *Do you need this*?

6. Do you find that your days are filled with managing what's urgent rather than pursuing what's important? What changes would create a better balance?

7. Think about what influences exist in your home that may be affecting your attentiveness to God. What are some known distractions?

8. Sometimes God uses several circumstances in combination to work in your life. Could the really difficult things going on in your life right now really be Him saying, "Come to Me"? How could God be jump-starting your faith right now?

DISCUSSION 4

Chapter 3
Delight to Obey: How God Grows
Our Desire to Follow Him

1. What are your favorite Bible stories? What are your kids' favorites?

2. When was the last time you got "lost" in reading the Bible—that is, you were so captivated you couldn't put it down? How and why did this happen, if it has happened?

3. What were your Bible reading habits while you were growing up? Did you ever read the Bible? Did your family read the Bible together? Do you have positive or negative memories related to spiritual things?

4. If your kids are older, what tips can you share with moms of younger children? If you could have some "Do Overs!" in your mothering, what would the most important ones be?

5. Dream a little. What would you like to see happen in your family in the next year as it relates to your hunger for God? In the next five years? In the next ten?

6. The book emphasizes moving beyond Bible reading as a habit to the goal of knowing Christ. How can taking it slowly be a positive element in Bible reading? Is your main aim truly to know Christ or is it something else? What do you think it is? Does it vary sometimes?

7. How can you grow to see Jesus and the gospel in all the pages of your Bible?

8. Read aloud this statement from chapter 3:

If they haven't spent time in God's Word, I want it to seem as if there's something not right about the day. But even more important, I want them to treasure God's Word. I want them to be able to say with the psalmist, "How sweet are Your words to my taste! Yes, sweeter than honey to my mouth!" (Psalm 119:103).

Pray for one another that this would be true for your kids' hearts—*and yours*!

DISCUSSION 5

Chapter 4
When the Going Gets Tough: How We Get through the Hard Passages

1. Read 2 Timothy 3:15. What implications does this have for our everyday lives?

2. Honesty check: What parts of the Bible just simply freak you out? Which parts trip you up? Which parts sound bizarre to your ears? *Can you imagine reading the Bible to your kids?*

3. Chapter 4 includes the statement that "the promise of Hebrews 4:12 is true: the Word of God is living and active, sometimes especially when it's hard for us to read or hear." Do you have any examples from your own life of how God's Word was active and effective, even though it was hard to accept?

4. When it comes to Bible reading, have you ever felt like saying, "Can we *please* read something else? He keeps saying the same thing over and over again"?

5. Have the kids shown you things about God that you couldn't see? Or has God used them to speak to you lately?

6. How can singing with your kids be powerful in helping teach your children truth from Scripture? How might it help make the things of God seem comfortable and natural in your home?

7. When your reading comes to issues of sexuality, how can you appropriate what you're reading and not pass it along verbatim? How might you handle stories of violence in Scripture?

8. Pray together, asking God to give you perseverance when you get into passages and seasons of life (or both at the same time!) that make it tough to keep reading the Bible.

DISCUSSION 6

Chapter 5
O God, You Are My God! What Happens When We Memorize God's Word

1. Did you grow up memorizing Bible verses? Are you memorizing now?

2. When it comes to the thought of adding in Scripture memorization to your already full plate, does it feel like an overwhelming thought to you?

3. Apart from any stress that may come into your mind as it relates to Scripture memorization, what joys might you expect? How might memorizing be transformative to you, your children, and your home?

4. If you were to start a new approach to memorizing today, do you know where you'd begin? Share some thinking with one another and help give one another fresh ideas. What part of Scripture might be a good place to begin?

5. How are you praying for your children and their salvation? How could memorizing Scripture help you as you pray for your kids?

6. On the day the author wanted to share Christ with her children, they were currently reading in Jeremiah—and she was able to use that chapter to talk about salvation. Do you have ideas about how you can use your everyday reading—no matter where you are in Scripture—to evangelize your children?

7. Share times when God's Word has spoken to you right when you needed it. Why does it have the power to do this?

8. Pray Colossians 3:16 (ESV) into your life:

Let the word of Christ dwell in you richly, teaching and admonishing one another in all wisdom, singing psalms and hymns and spiritual songs, with thankfulness in your hearts to God.

DISCUSSION 7

Chapter 6

Sovereign Timing: How God Continually Orchestrated Our Reading

1. Read Romans 8:31–39. What do these verses say about God? His character and ways? What do they say about us? Who is for us? What is able to separate us from Christ's love?

2. Do you feel confident that the Father loves you and is working all things together for your good? Why or why not?

3. Carrie shares the story of how God timed for her and the kids to read certain verses on certain days. How can you tell this was not coincidental?

4. Do you look forward to each day and have expectancy that God is eager to speak to you?

5. Share times when God has used Scripture to confirm a decision you were making. When has God used His Word to reveal that you were not making the right decision? How did you respond?

6. What Scriptures come to mind regarding God and His providential care?

7. How do we train ourselves—and our kids—to recognize that the Father really does love us and works all things together for our good?

8. Thank God for working all things together for your good—and count on Him afresh today!

DISCUSSION 8

Chapter 7
We Did It! You Can, Too

1. There are plenty of difficult places in Scripture. Have you developed a strategy for when you hit them?

2. Carrie used a commentary to catch the drift of what was going on in Revelation. What tools have been helpful in discovering what the original point of a passage is or how *rightly* to apply it to us today?

3. Do you seek your husband's input and advice regarding the Bible or your reading of God's Word? How can you affirm his leadership in a practical way?

4. Do you know of any parents who have read the entire Bible with their children? Are there any "distinctives" about this family?

5. What do you know about the state of biblical literacy today? Do you think this generation knows its Bible as well as the previous generation did?

6. What does Carrie mean when she says, "God did not open up His Word to us because of who we are. He spoke to us through His Word because of who He is"?

7. How do you feel about the possibility of you making it through God's Word—in its entirety? If it happens, would it be an "act of God"?

8. Would you be willing to make a commitment—realizing that grace abounds!—to read the Bible with your kids, for your sake and for theirs? What concerns you about making a commitment?

DISCUSSION 9

Chapter 8
Sweeter than Honey: Lessons I Learned

1. If your aim in Bible reading is to know God, how does this relieve the pressure to read quickly, well, or in large amounts?

2. When you think about the word *accountability*, do you cringe? Why or why not? How can reading to children provide positive accountability to your Bible reading?

3. Do you use mealtimes to the best advantage? What are a couple of ways that you might be more intentional in bringing a spiritual focus into your everyday routine?

4. Name some of the practical benefits to reading out loud. How can God use reading aloud to deepen your love for Him and His Word?

5. Are your Bible reading times fun? Do you need to lighten up? Do you need prayer support right now?

6. Read Deuteronomy 6:7. How does this round-the-clock teaching work in your family? Do you need some group-think time to help you get more creative?

7. If you miss a day of reading, do you have pangs of guilt? Why or why not?

8. Pray that God would help you and your kids believe His Word and that He would use Scripture to change each of you into the image of Christ.

DISCUSSION 10

Chapter 9

What Next? What Happens
When We Cross the Finish Line

1. Why was jumping right back into Genesis 1—and not taking a break from Bible reading—a good idea for Carrie?

2. What are some principles for choosing a good translation? What are you using right now?

3. Read Nehemiah 8:9. Carrie writes, "When the people heard God's Word, they understood what He required and that they didn't measure up—and they cried. I could relate." Can you relate?

4. Is the Lord doing a new work in your heart? Do you have new desires to get to know God through His

Word? Do you ever rejoice over just understanding what you read in your Bible today?

5. Philippians 1:6 says, "He who began a good work in you will perfect it until the day of Christ Jesus." Take some time to pray, right now, that a genuine appetite to grow would be in your heart. Thank God for this promise.

6. Do you struggle with comparing yourself to other women and mothers?

7. Talk about how influential mothers are in their children's lives, especially during the years they are still living at home. How many years will your children probably still live with you? What are the best ways you want to influence them?

8. Read aloud the passages of Scripture listed on pages 141–42 (Psalms 19:7–8; 119:11, 105; John 17:17; Romans 10:17; 2 Timothy 3:16–17; and Hebrews 4:12). Consider and then discuss what God's Word can do in our lives.

Translation Comparison

SO MANY BIBLE TRANSLATIONS
A Guide to Help

Translation/Paraphrase	2 Timothy 3:16
KJV	All scripture is given by inspiration of God, and is profitable for doctrine, for reproof, for correction, for instruction in righteousness.
NASB	All Scripture is inspired by God and profitable for teaching, for reproof, for correction, for training in righteousness.

ESV	All Scripture is breathed out by God and profitable for teaching, for reproof, for correction, and for training in righteousness.
HCSB	All Scripture is inspired by God and is profitable for teaching, for rebuking, for correcting, for training in righteousness.
NLT	All Scripture is inspired by God and is useful to teach us what is true and to make us realize what is wrong in our lives. It corrects us when we are wrong and teaches us to do what is right.
NIV	All Scripture is God-breathed and is useful for teaching, rebuking, correcting and training in righteousness.
NCV	All Scripture is inspired by God and is useful for teaching, for showing people what is wrong in their lives, for correcting faults, and for teaching how to live right.

Amplified

Every Scripture is God-breathed (given by His inspiration) and profitable for instruction, for reproof and conviction of sin, for correction of error and discipline in obedience, [and] for training in righteousness (in holy living, in conformity to God's will in thought, purpose, and action).

The Message

But don't let it faze you. Stick with what you learned and believed, sure of the integrity of your teachers— why, you took in the sacred Scriptures with your mother's milk! There's nothing like the written Word of God for showing you the way to salvation through faith in Christ Jesus. Every part of Scripture is God-breathed and useful one way or another— showing us truth, exposing our rebellion, correcting our mistakes, training us to live God's way. Through the Word we are put together and shaped up for the tasks God has for us.

Everyday dads, your mission is to love and enjoy God and make Him known to your family. Here are some thoughts to help you join your bride in pursuing Jesus together.

Seek to draw near to God personally through Bible reading, study, and prayer.

Your wife and kids need you to love God and treasure Him above everything else—even them. Get to know Him on your own and with them. Pick up your Bible and read, or listen to the Bible on audio in the car. Talk to God throughout the day. Enjoy pursuing God.

**Seek to create an open atmosphere that
gives your family ample opportunity
to talk with you about God.**

Create a climate that says, "It's okay to talk about God here!" Be sure not to relegate "God-talk" to just certain times. It'll get awkward fast that way. Make talking about God comfortable all day long. Don't force it.

**Lead and direct your family in seeking
God through Bible study and prayer.**

You can continue to find times to read the Bible with your wife and kids even if your wife is reading to the kids. Also, encourage family members to seek God on their own, according to their abilities. Be the man who says, "Hey everyone, listen to what I'm learning here" and "Let's talk to God about what we're going through." Talk about the Lord and with the Lord often.

**Encourage and pray for your wife as she directs
your children toward God and His Word.**

If your wife is reading with the kids, be a huge cheerleader of those special times. Don't get jealous. Work together to point your kids to Christ. Ask God to bless her efforts. Be your wife's biggest fan. Take her needs to the Lord in prayer.

Be willing to admit you don't
have all the answers.

Why? Because you don't! Don't become the "Bible Answer Man." Even if you know a lot, use your wisdom with grace and love. Help find answers, love your wife in an understanding way, and don't provoke your kids. Let them hear you say, "I don't know, but I will find out" and then let them see you dig in and find answers—humbly.

Seek the answers when questions come.

As the leader in your home, stay in training. As believers, we're to be lifelong learners. As a dad, you'll be a lifelong teacher, too. Diligently dig for answers. If you don't know how to do this well, talk to your pastor or other Bible teacher. Be bold enough to be humble, and ask for help if you need it.

Spend time with your family—
as a group and one-on-one.

Be intentional about spending as much time as you can with your family. Carve out time for each member to get some personal time with you. Just enjoy them. Quantity and quality time build bridges to your heart—and yours to theirs—like nothing else can.

Pray out loud for your wife and kids.

No one knows your wife and children like you do. As

you get in the habit of taking them to the throne of grace in private, also let them hear you talk to God about them. Let them hear how you're praying for their hearts, their days, their future mates, their friends, their place in the world, and more. Pray about the tiniest of details in great detail. It matters.

Seek to protect their spiritual well-being.

Scripture contains many commands about husbands and wives and children. Learn them. Fight for the spiritual health of your home. Provide thoughtful space to your wife and children to help them come to Christ and center their lives on Him and the gospel. If there is anything attacking or eroding their pursuit of Jesus, get proactive and go to work in protecting them. No one is going to protect them like you can and should.

Resist the urge to give up.

When you fail (and you will) and when your wife doesn't always respond as you hope (and she won't) and you get discouraged in some other way (it'll happen), resist, resist, resist the urge to shut down and throw in the towel. Find friends or a pastor to encourage you when it's hard. But, no matter what, don't stop seeking God's heart and the heart of your wife and kids—and don't stop loving them like crazy. It's worth it. Stay faithful to the finish. By God's help, you can do it.

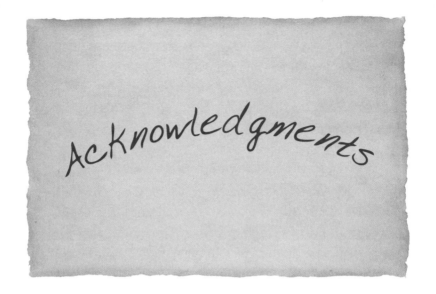

Acknowledgments

Wes, I love sharing life's adventures with you. Thank you for your sacrificial love for me and for the numerous hats you have so adeptly worn in the making of this book. Graham, Maggie, Benjamin, and Emma, God is central in this book, but He has given you supporting roles. Thank you for teaching me about enjoying God and responding quickly to His Word. I am honored to be your mom. Thank you for the sacrifices you have made so that I could "go write" and for letting me tell stories about you when you were much younger.

Thank you John and Patricia Murphy (Mom and Dad), for your love, generosity, and faithfulness to each other and your family. I could not have asked for better parents. I love you! Thank you, Joe and Evelyn Ward, for raising a good son. Thank you for loving and encouraging him (and his family).

Thank you Nancy Leigh DeMoss, for the ways you have influenced us. Your impact is evident throughout this book. Thank you Paula Hendricks, Sandy Bixel, Carrie Gaul, Sandra Hawkins, Hugh and Renae Duncan, and Brian and Holly Hedges, for being early (and insightful!) readers and encouragers. Thanks for your careful review, perceptive input, and steadfast prayers. Thank you Cheryl Dunlop Molin, for your helpful early edit.

Thank you Salzmans, Harveys, Newells, Hwangs, and Guinns, for repeatedly listening to book prayer requests and for praying and supporting me. To the many other praying friends (too many to name), thank you for going before God on my behalf and expressing timely encouragement.

To the Moody team, thank you for your desire to publish books that draw us to God. Thanks Greg Thornton, for giving this book a second look and seeing God's hand in our story. Holly Kisly, I am so thankful for your tireless work, your kindness to me personally, and your sincere desire to see moms and kids discover God's Word. Thank you Annette LaPlaca, for skillful editing, your encouraging and responsive nature, and for being a mom who wants to see her children love Jesus. Thank you Maralynn Rochat, for your creative heart and hand that gave us the whimsical birds.

Thank You, Lord. I know that I am an unlikely candidate to write a book about reading the Bible. Thank You for lovingly pursuing me, opening Your Word to me, and giving me this opportunity to share what You have done.

A **true wͦman** BOOK

The goal of the **True Woman** publishing line is to encourage women to:

- Discover, embrace, and delight in God's divine design and mission for their lives
- Reflect the beauty and heart of Jesus Christ to their world
- Intentionally pass the baton of Truth on to the next generation
- Pray earnestly for an outpouring of God's Spirit in their families, churches, nation and world

To learn more about the **True Woman movement** and the many resources available for individuals, small groups, and local church women's ministries, visit us online:

- www.ReviveOurHearts.com
- www.TrueWoman.com
- www.LiesYoungWomenBelieve.com

The **True Woman Manifesto** summarizes the core beliefs at the heart of this movement. You can sign the manifesto, find a downloadable PDF, and order additional copies at:

- www.Truewoman.com/Manifesto

True Woman is an outreach of:

Revive Our Hearts

Calling women to freedom, fullness, and fruitfulness in Christ

P.O. Box 2000 | Niles, MI 49120